LAST TRAIN TO PARADISE

Also by Graham Hutchins:

Great New Zealand Railway Journeys (Exisle 2008)

Eight Days A Week (Exisle 2004)

LAST TRAIN TO PARADISE

Journeys from the Golden Age of New Zealand Railways

GRAHAM HUTCHINS

EXISLE PUBLISHING

First published 2011

Exisle Publishing Limited,
P.O. Box 60-490, Titirangi, Auckland 0642, New Zealand.
'Moonrising', Narone Creek Road, Wollombi, NSW 2325, Australia.
www.exislepublishing.com

National Library of New Zealand Cataloguing-in-Publication Data

Hutchins, Graham.
Last train to paradise : journeys from the golden age of
New Zealand railways / Graham Hutchins.
Includes bibliographical references.
ISBN 978-0-908988-68-6
1. Railroads—New Zealand—History. 2. Railroad travel—
New Zealand—History. I. Title.
385.0993—dc 22

10 9 8 7 6 5 4 3 2 1

Text design and production by IslandBridge
Cover design by Dexter Fry
Printed in Singapore by KHL Printing Co Pte Ltd
This book uses paper sourced under ISO 14001 guidelines
from well-managed forests and other controlled sources.

Contents

OND CLASS

Introduction

Last Train to Paradise is a celebratory account of a time when train travel was more than just the accepted means of travelling around New Zealand. It was also an era when rail journeys provided excitement, companionship and a certain romance.

In those days almost everyone — royal visitors, politicians, Governors General, businessmen, farmers, public servants, entertainers, writers, sports teams, soldiers off to war, overseas tourists, local holidaymakers, commuters, casual travellers, even prison escapers on the run and other freeloaders — travelled by train. At a time when cars were thin on the ground and roads often little more than gravelled goat tracks, the railways were both pivotal and prestigious.

A high sense of communality prevailed during the golden age of train travel, unlike the fragmented and individualistic era of the motorcar in more recent times. In many ways *Last Train to Paradise* covers a slice of New Zealand history when Kiwis were on their best behaviour. Mostly.

With railway stations often the hub of towns served by trains and city rail citadels Mecca for thousands of travellers, railway journeys were more than just a means of getting from A to B. 'Name' trains, the likes of the Rotorua Limited, Opua Express and South Island Express, held pride of place, with the journey being as intriguing as the destination.

In general terms the first 50 or so years of the twentieth century have often been considered the golden age, although, in terms of the significance of rail travel, the period from 1880 to 1960 was probably more representative. As well as becoming established as the principal means of transporting freight, the railways held sway then as the most popular — and often the only — way New Zealanders moved around. Suburban trains flourished. Special excursion jaunts were common. Trains took you to work and home again, or to special events as leisure time increased. Kids went to school by train. Mothers and grandmothers went to town. Royal trains, troop trains, test-match specials, and other such excursions, each had an aura of their own.

More than anything though, 'name' trains of the era held a special fascination, as train travel emerged from earlier decades in the developing

Previous page

Don't spare the horses. Two engines – K 911 and J 1227 – haul the Auckland to Wellington Express in 1949.

J.A.T. Terry Photo

Harry Lauder, the Scottish singer resplendent in kilt and sporran, stands on the cowcatcher of a Q engine amidst dignitaries and admirers. His rakish gait confirms the affectionate connection between train travel and visiting entertainers during the halcyon years of New Zealand passenger trains.

J.A.T. Terry Collection

colony, when trains were seen as a novelty. Long and middle-distance expresses and limiteds were glorified by some, although it took their diminution in later years for many New Zealanders to appreciate what they had lost.

Last Train to Paradise celebrates the old passenger trains that roared and swayed through a different New Zealand. If a time machine were at our disposal it would be tempting to go back to the days of steam-drawn services and less complicated ways and take a seat on a train heading out. Out of strangulating big cities, tedious small towns and away from lonely backwaters and rural haunts, when there was always the promise of better things down the line.

Trains held the hope of escape. As the ubiquitous AB engines propelled earlier trains and the altogether more overbearing Ks and KAs bullied their way to the front in later years, the spectre of the looming railcar years seemed too distant to contemplate. The Js and JAs, more sleek and elegant, also held pride of place at the head of the train.

Trains not only linked communities, they were communities in themselves. The stations were their temples, where every man and his dog, every woman in her finery, every farmer in gumboots, every child in school kit and every trooper in sandpaper-rough uniform, gathered either to welcome or farewell someone, or take their place on board.

New Zealand was a different place. While there were wars and a depression to endure, and an egalitarianism that often curdled into arch-conservatism, back then graffiti was some brave soldier emblazoning his troop train carriage with 'We're off to beat Mussolini' in chalk, or a happy drunk daubing 'Merry Xmas' on the Newmarket signal box. Social mayhem was a gaggle of rugby supporters making a lot of noise on the platform and even more once on board. Trains ran through communities built on a sound foundation. Men worked, women were home-makers and mothers, and kids knew their place, which by today's standards, was in the sun. Self-esteem would have sounded as if it was vaguely related to the means of propulsion at the head of the trains.

Off to war — again. Kiwi soldiers put on a brave face as their troop train prepares to depart. Some never came home.

ATL-1/2-061218-F

My generation grew up to the sound of trains, and once we'd realised that the surviving services in the 1950s were not the melting tip of the iceberg, but its rapidly diminishing remains, we began looking back. Back to days when passenger trains were everywhere and everyone took them — often for granted — as a means of conveyance and communality.

Last Train to Paradise is unashamedly nostalgic. Many of us would like to go back and travel at a different pace and to a different place, where we would once again know where we stood in the Kiwi scheme of things, and sing the praises of a more certain social setting.

The old trains were like revered friends. We used to count the number of carriages on the Auckland – Wellington Express and we memorised the numbers of the AB, KA and JA engines. Such rituals represented a profound respect for something we figured was here to stay. It never occurred to us that one day such omnipresent people-movers would fade from the landscape. And of course we waved at the trains. Sometimes passengers waved back, although as the 50s merged into the 60s, fewer did.

Then we stopped waving. Trains became passé, unfashionable. The motorcar emerged as the chariot of gods and ordinary jokers, and all too frequently, they were chariots of fire and destruction. The outer facades of the trains began to fade. New car owners saw them as a grubby blot on the landscape, an encumbrance to bear at level crossings. Gone were the days of bright, gleaming engines and sleek, polished carriages, when the sight of a train produced excitement and yearning, with more than a hint of a world of intrigue and fascination.

Last Train to Paradise also visits the people who travelled on the old trains. Joe Blow and his wife and kids were familiar enough, but the trains also carried celebrities. Royalty had their own designated trains, personalities like Paderewski, the world-famous Polish pianist, had special carriages given over to their ease of passage. Then there were those celebrities who simply bought a ticket and took their chances, just like the rest of us. Mark Twain, the famous American author, took a New Zealand train back in the 1890s:

November 11. On the road. The train-express goes twenty and one-half miles an hour, schedule time; but it is fast enough, the outlook upon sea and land is so interesting, and the cars so comfortable. They are not English and not American; they are the Swiss combination of the two. A narrow and railed porch along the side, where a person can walk up and down. A lavatory in each car. This is progress, this is nineteenth century spirit. In New Zealand, these fast expresses run twice a week. It is well to know this if you want to be a bird and fly through the country at a 20-mile gait; otherwise you might start on one of the five wrong days, and then you will get a train that can't overtake its own shadow.[1]

Rudyard Kipling, the Anglo-Indian author, was an early traveller on New Zealand trains.

ATL-PAColl-0070

Rudyard Kipling, the much loved Anglo-Indian author, also travelled on New Zealand trains. He was less complimentary about their speed, although he enjoyed the ride, wrote a reporter with the *Star* newspaper.

During the journey to Christchurch, he [Kipling] conversed with those near him and showed a lively interest in the country we were passing through, especially praising the Heathcote river and the rich land. He was not complimentary, however, to the speed attained by the train, and in fact said he knew of only one country where the pace was slower. Arrived in Christchurch he confided to me that he required just then but two things, a cigar and a shave.[2]

Beyond the nineteenth century the trains had sped up. Sadly, the trappings of progress had seen the likes of Paderewski sequestered away in his own carriage. It was a pity the famous Pole could not share his rapier wit with fellow passengers, in the manner of Twain and Kipling. Paderewski had once been introduced to a polo player and summed up the situation in a twinkling: 'You are a dear soul who plays polo, and I am a poor Pole who plays solo.'[3]

The trains never wanted for humour and bonhomie. When the London Gaiety Burlesque Company toured the country, trains carried the emissaries of fun and frivolity to various centres. Special excursion trains, in turn, transported high-spirited locals to the troupe's many performances of *Miss Esmerelda,* a popular favourite.

When J. L. Toole, 'England's greatest comedian', toured New Zealand with his company, the *Manawatu Herald* recorded a certain hilarity associated with the famous visitor's departure by train.

> Among the passengers yesterday, were Messrs Krull and Poole, besides Mr J. L. Toole. As the train was leaving the station, Mr Krull intended to call for three cheers for the great comedian but in the flurry of the moment gave the name of Poole instead of Toole. Needless to say the crowd immediately gave three vociferous cheers, which our local sport acknowledged by bowing and raising his hat. Somebody remarked that it was 'Krull' of Poole to take advantage of Toole.[4]

In later years it was possible to detect a general light-heartedness among our own folk — celebrities and otherwise — when the time came to take the train.

Writer Robin Hyde, using her real name of Iris Wilkinson, in the *New Zealand Railways Magazine*, described the liberating properties of train travel when visiting exciting destinations.

> When people said to me, 'Have you heard about the Glow-Worm Grotto?' I answered 'Aha, but have you heard the one about the Scotchman who met the Irishman, when the both of them were going to market?' or words to that effect. However there was a weekend excursion, and Auckland had taken on a sudden look of frightfulness, and the only place in the city that I could bear to look at, at all, was that handsome bronze, buff and green railway station. So the next thing was to my own surprise, I was on a train bound for the Waitomo Caves, and feeling curiously thrilled about it, but prepared to be disappointed.

> It was a good train, too . . . a good many others had had the same idea about spending a weekend as myself, including a party of Australians whose great pet was a large stuffed wallaby with a pink smile on his face. There were also footballers, playing the ukulele and crooning in a nearby carriage: and by and by, a pretty lass came through, and with an earnest expression on her face said, 'Come along and see, it's a treasure hunt.' After that the journey took on an extraordinarily sociable, and at the same time very active character, people crawling about looking under the pillows of the few old stagers who, far from joining in, had gone peacefully off to sleep, sprawling back in the deep leather-cushioned chairs. But we all survived the treasure hunt, even the wallaby, in whose pouch, as it turned out, they had hidden the treasure; and after a light lunch and more cursory refreshments at minor ports of call, we arrived with a wild Redskin whoop (that was partly the train's whistle and partly the footballers) at a tiny station called Hangatiki.[5]

The first 'snow train' to National Park in 1938 produced as much fun and fascination. It was debatable if the destination point — the mountains of the central plateau of the North Island — produced more pleasant memories than the train journey itself. 'Slalom', writing in the *New Zealand Railways Magazine,* captured the light-heartedness engendered by the much-loved 'snow train'.

> 'Sno' good', punned one wit as he left the train at Wellington the following morning and his humorous dejection at the thought of the weekend finished, surely had its counterpart in the minds of others.[6]

'Manuhiri', writing in the same magazine, described the more earthy elements of passenger travel through rugged hinterlands. The journeys were no less enjoyable.

> It had been sale day in Taihape, and some of these hard-boiled sons of the soil journeying homeward by train had reached the state described in his

> poem, 'Tam O'Shanter' by Robbie Burns. 'The night drave on wi sangs and clatter ay the ale was growing better.' [7]

The people on board were as diverting as the power and presence of the trains, as they sped through matchless landscapes. They were history-makers as they went about their daily business, bringing with them vestiges and reminders of societal forces. It wasn't just the men on troop trains that represented a world — and country — at war. Nor was it just the drunks and hobos, stowing away in vestibule and toilet, who felt the bite of hard times and depression.

Then there was the history of the trains themselves. Train travel invariably invites contemplation, as aspects of what went before surfaces. The origin of the lines, the evolution of the different types of trains and the red-letter days of rail celebrations and line openings. Inevitably tales of tragedy and mishap also emerged. Sadness impinged, as in the time author Janet Frame welcomed home a dear departed sister's coffin at Oamaru Station. Then there was Tangiwai. My family and I travelled on the Auckland – Wellington Express two years after the famous disaster. A tingle of dread accompanied our crossing of the Whangaehu River where 151 people died.

In lieu of having had the privilege of travelling on the older trains, I have approached the project from the standpoint of single, organic journeys traced on specific days in specific years. These have been fleshed out with accounts of those who were lucky enough to have travelled on the trains, and the insertions of keen observers provide a voice for those special times, as the old train journeys return to the mind's landscape.

In later years I travelled on passenger services that still trundled down the path of the famous old trains. Sadly the Northerner, Southerner, Silver Fern, Silver Star and other modern services couldn't replicate the character and excitement of a bygone era, and provincial railcars didn't have the

The Silver Star, introduced in 1971, was a brave attempt to usher in a new age of sophisticated rail travel: an all-sleeper service on the Auckland-Wellington route.

D.R. Simpson

glamour and significance of the old trains. While I'm only too aware that the mixed trains, in their death throes, were often like grubby museum pieces, all the passenger services beyond the golden era that coincided with my emergence as a rail fan were much sought after. Their often unfashionable meanderings were rendered profound by the fact that the famous old trains once used the same lines as their stamping ground.

Finally, trains like the TranzAlpine and Overlander introduced a new sophistication, far removed from the omnipresent, bustling services of the golden era. These modern trains, in another, market-driven New Zealand, were expected to make a financial profit as they plugged into the tourist boom. Again, I went along for the new ride, realising that such services covered the tracks — in more ways than one — of their precursors, the famous old trains. Through a New Zealand that has changed forever, if not for the better.

1 Sleepless in Taihape

The Auckland – Wellington Express, 1955

> There is now a railway in course of construction from Auckland to Mercer and from thence there is water-carriage by the two rivers to Cambridge and Alexandra [Pirongia]. That the colony can afford to make these railways, I will not take upon myself to say. The making of them is part of that grand go-ahead policy of which Mr Vogel is the eminent professor. That the Waikato district will be benefited by the railway when it is made there can be no doubt whatever.

In this way English writer, Anthony Trollope, in 1872 (as recorded by A. H. Reed in his later re-edition of Trollope's work entitled *With Anthony Trollope in New Zealand*), presaged the looming significance of the first northern link in the North Island Main Trunk railway. Thirty years later the line was still well short of completion but the 'grand go-ahead policy' Trollope identified would eventually see the line completed in 1908 and the passage of the Auckland to Wellington express secured.[1]

From the day the first Auckland to Wellington train ran in 1909, a mystique developed and the Auckland – Wellington Express was on its way into the hearts and minds of New Zealanders. The romance of the railways soon blossomed into a deeply passionate relationship as the express became a cornerstone of a developing nation.

My love affair with trains began with the Auckland to Wellington Express, and the return service from the capital to the Queen City, seen through the eyes of an infatuated young boy, one of many who were drawn to it. Like some steam-driven rooster, the express engines would wake you in the morning as they set out for Auckland and in the evening as night fell on Te Kuiti, they'd keep a watching brief on our valley as they headed south into that vast unknown territory. Here, under cover of darkness, the express climbed mountains, went up and down spirals, disappeared for hours into long tunnels and crossed viaducts as tall as the Eiffel Tower. One day we would see for ourselves, although we remembered the limitations of trying to see in the dark.

Te Kuiti in the 1950s was the consummate railway settlement. It was my hometown and I grew up to the sound of steam engines chortling as

Previous page

The Auckland-Wellington Express, behind engine number JA 1276, near Frankton in 1959.

J.A.T. Terry Photo

Every man and his dog had his day on the old Express. The porter at this station has his work cut out.

HCL-05271 (Roose Collection)

they approached the station from the north, along the last vestiges of the low-lying rail corridor across the plains, or hammering as they protested up the steep bank beyond the town to the south, where the King Country hills closed in. Trains heading north were less obtrusive.

The Auckland to Wellington Express may have been a transitory visitor, but its presence galvanised the town. In 1955 it was the most popular of the passenger trains, and it had already had a similar effect on other small towns back up the track by the time it reached Te Kuiti, after leaving Auckland at 3pm on a cloudy afternoon.

Although the express didn't enter service until 1909, after the main trunk was finally completed in 1908, it rapidly assumed an aura few other New Zealand trains could muster. It covered the greatest distance of any single long-distance service, linking New Zealand's two largest cities. In the days before roads were deemed adequate as a link between our major city, Auckland, and the capital, and before air travel was viable or affordable, people gravitated to the service, as if coaxed by the Pied Piper wailing of the big K and KA engines. Or the Js and JAs, if they had taken up the assignment.

The departure of the express from Auckland station, one Friday afternoon in 1955, was typically boisterous. Friday was invariably a popular day to travel. University students and school kids turned their backs on institutions of learning and returned to hometowns down the line for the weekend, and Aucklanders quit their city for others such as Hamilton and Wellington, or the ski resorts accessible via National Park. Troops travelled to Waiouru Army camp; rugby teams and supporters were off to play and heckle down-country opponents; farmers returned to the wide open spaces after a day in the big smoke, and family groups took the train to visit country cousins.

'The train', for North Islanders, even in 1955, was invariably the Auckland to Wellington Express. While other services plied pleasant provincial runs, the express took on a workman-like urgency as it hammered through the heart and centre of the country. Over the years Governors General, Prime Ministers and VIPs used the train, with vice-regal cars, especially designated for the Governor-General, attached to the rear of the express.

Celebrities and living legends took their places with faces you'd never seen before. All Blacks were often sighted. Usually they'd merge with the mainstream masses and queue at refreshment rooms and fight for sleep as the train plunged through the other side of midnight, just like everyone else. Once, not long after World War II, All Black Jack Finlay injured himself running into an open window on Frankton Station while joining the refreshment room stampede. He missed a test match because of the blow, but no doubt still had his pie and cuppa.

At 3pm the express, pulled by a JA engine, announced its intentions. These days some trains move silently out of the terminus, but the JA hissed and roared and blasted on its whistle as it felt the weight of a long train. Out on the Waitemata Harbour boats and ferries plied the choppy waters as the line followed Tamaki Drive until it crossed the causeway linking Judges Bay, Hobson Bay and the Orakei Basin.

In earlier times the express used to leave from the old Auckland Station, and was obliged to climb the Parnell bank and overbridge before continuing to climb along the old route that carried on through Newmarket, before finding an easier camber through Greenlane and Ellerslie to the south. In 1930 the new Auckland Station had been completed, an impressive building that inevitably added to the lustre of the express, with its cafeterias, shops and cavernous halls echoing the excited voices of passengers making their way to the platform. The new Westfield Deviation along the waterfront opened the same year.

As the train swooshed across the causeway on its way south, older, experienced travellers marvelled at both the maritime aspect and the speed mustered by a train that no longer had to labour up the old line towards Parnell. An air of excitement saw several passengers moving about the train even before the guard had clipped their tickets.

Rail citadel for departing passengers. Auckland Railway Station with Waitemata Harbour beyond.

ATL-1/2-071820-F

The driver had the eastern reaches of the city to himself, in the sense that the new Westfield Deviation, all 16 km of it, was no longer hindered by the need for caution at level road crossings. There were none. Overbridges and underpasses contributed to a swift dispatch.

Beyond the bays and inlets of the Waitemata the line arced towards the southwest, after giving those of the passengers who were travelling on the train for the first time an additional thrill. The Purewa Tunnel, 596 m long, was unexpected and children made various noises of exclamation. Women, still moving around the carriage, expressed a combination of delighted surprise and guarded concern, should the tunnel go on for too long and leave them 'loitering' in the dark, largely unaccounted for, with strange men on either side of them. Thoughts of a much-touted promotional poster boasting of 'the romance of the railways' swirled in their heads, inducing a sense of forbidden excitement to go with the guarded concern.

The train soon emerged into the light and headed through Glen Innes towards the junction with the old line at Westfield, fringing Auckland's other harbour, the Manukau. After the beauty of the Waitemata, the Manukau presents a grimmer visage. Rain squalls suddenly dash against the windows as the train turns south through a grubby, industrial enclave. The freezing works belch out unpleasant odours that filter into the train through those windows not already closed against the rain. Westfield, one of New Zealand's 'killing capitals' where livestock from the farms are dispatched, reminds travellers of the unpleasant side of an agricultural nation, as bilge from the works oozes onto already scruffy mudflats at the northern end of the harbour.

Some passengers prefer to disregard the blotchy industrial landscape, choosing instead to catch up on the headlines in the *New Zealand Herald*, or engage in banter with fellow travellers. A recurring conversation piece is the fact that New Zealand's largest city has two rail approach routes from the south. Folks marvel at the extravagance, set against New Zealand Railway's apparent frugality in such matters.

Off in the distance, shrouded in mist, the Onehunga road bridge reveals cars flitting like ants scurrying across a kitchen bench when the sugar has been spilt. The wind cuts in off the Manukau and another shower of rain comes seemingly from nowhere, out of an almost clear sky. It's that time of year when clouds are buffeted along by brisk breezes and dump their moisture 'out of the blue'.

Through Otahuhu and Papatoetoe evidence of Auckland's southern suburban sprawl stretches away on both sides of the track, while beyond Manurewa and Papakura, open green spaces survive the encroachment. The express speeds towards Paerata, a junction settlement. Seven years earlier it was still possible to travel due west from here on a mixed train bound for Waiuku, until 1948, when the service was terminated.

The Auckland to Wellington Express is a night train. In winter the light begins to fade and the temperature drops as the line catches up with the Waikato River. Further on the track passes through the Whangamarino wetlands, in 1914 the scene of an accident involving the express. A goods train had been shunting wagons from the main line on to a siding, but some wagons were still on the right of way. Despite this, the express was given a green light. Several months before, a workman had replaced a wheel in the signalling mechanism with one smaller than it should have been. Unwisely, the signal wires were tightened to compensate for the smaller wheel. The night of the accident was the winter's first severe cold snap, causing the wire to contract and yank the signal into the proceed position, with a green light pulsing.

The express collided with the wagons. A mail van immediately behind the engine telescoped into the following sleeping car. Three travellers were killed and five seriously injured. Those who lost their lives were Mr G. N. Grimstone, registrar of the Tokerau Native Land Court, Mr Orton Stevens, New Zealand manager of the National Mutual Life Association of Australasia, and Mr Charles Peterson of Melbourne. It was a dark moment in the history of the express and for the Whangamarino settlement. The tablet-porter at the station was considered to have been remiss in not checking the signal more frequently and was charged with negligence and manslaughter, although he was later acquitted.

Splintered carriages, shattered lives. The Express all askew at Whangamarino, 1914.

J.A.T. Terry Collection

In 1955 the watery winter light was fading further as the train passed through Huntly and Ngaruawahia, and the lights of Hamilton were blinking as Frankton Junction greeted the express. Frankton was bustling and brightly lit in the gathering gloom. Long gone are tales of it being the hub of 'white slave traffic' with young women off the trains abducted and coerced into prostitution, and shifty men lurking around shadowy corners. There may have been more concerns, in the conservative 1950s, about reports of girls visiting the railway huts for the pleasure of single railway labourers, but on the station there are no more drunks and loiterers than you'd expect to find on a Friday evening. Some were even waiting to catch the express.

Catherine Hill, a local identity who became known as 'Coffee and Bun', would have been amongst the swirling rabble on the platform in the years after World War II. Speculation set in as to why she frequented the station so regularly for many years. Some suggested she was checking out the trains for a fiancé who never made it home from World War I, others that she was simply lonely and enjoyed the lift from the sudden and transitory infusion of through-passengers. Perhaps she enjoyed the diversity but didn't need to get too close; they were soon off down the line once a fresh engine was attached and the 'all aboard' sounded.

As night closed in, the Auckland to Wellington Express entered the territory and time zone that defined its modus operandi: the hills, plateaux and mountains of the central North Island as the northern plains receded; and the hours of darkness.

Thousands of New Zealanders had their own stories to tell of the Auckland to Wellington Express. Their own reasons for catching it, their own boarding point, their own town, their own unique experiences. In Te Kuiti, I grew up with the notion that the Auckland to Wellington Express was the principal means of getting anywhere.

One Friday evening in 1955, my family and I were off to Wellington to stay with friends and family. My kid sister was staying with my grandmother back in Te Kuiti, leaving me, my other sister and Mum and Dad to take the train. It would be our first time travelling south together on the express from Te Kuiti, although we'd all become familiar with the early morning journey north to Auckland.

We'd also become familiar with the 'towns within towns' associated with several railway settlements along the main trunk, those clusters of distinctive railway houses where railway workers and their families lived.

Railway towns were an integral part of the Kiwi landscape during the golden age, with their unique architecture, commonality of function and purpose and the need for daytime silence as night-drivers and workers slept.

We acknowledged the importance of Te Kuiti's Railway Town, in the heyday of the Auckland to Wellington Express, as readily as we did the need for ribbon-development with shops down one side of the street, the better to accommodate the main trunk railway. Back up the track, Te Kuiti's Railway Town was a vital, ready-made suburb in a town of four thousand people. Railway Town had its own grocery on the corner, a sporting complex and rugby field with goalposts higher than Te Kuiti's principal rugby field.

The people were different too. Like the farmers, the residents of Railway Town often seemed a little removed from the small-town merchants and public servants. In all my years growing up in Te Kuiti, I only visited a house in Railway Town once, when the son of an engine driver invited me to his Frankton-built, rimu-framed railway house. We heard a lot of untoward stuff about Railway Town, based largely on ignorance of the place: grog, wantonness, even anti-royal sentiments and couples living together under the shadow of non-marital non-bliss. There were gang-like congregations along the Mangaoekewa River, where fishing for eels was as prevalent as riverbank groping, as puberty descended and the Auckland to Wellington Express passed through on the opposite bank, very much on time. In truth, Railway Town was more cohesive and disciplined than other parts of town. It had to be. The occupants and their families were responsible for overseeing and supporting an often dangerous work environment and the safety of thousands of travellers.

Timekeeping was critical, and the expresses didn't mangle schedules on the basically flat stretch between Auckland and Te Kuiti. It was more common to see Wellington to Auckland services struggling to make up time, after grappling with the central North Island high country, the Raurimu Spiral, and the broken territory beyond Taumarunui.

Night has all but fallen on Te Kuiti as passengers muddle around and huddle together, seeking the best stretch of platform, and trying to keep out the wind. Sheep-like shuffles see the knot of passengers move towards the spot where they hope their carriage will come to rest. There have been reports that the express sometimes drags its cars beyond the platform, so the engine comes to rest directly beneath the water vats. If that's the case on this occasion, it may mean an awkward climb from the shingle to the carriage steps.

Young bucks warm to that challenge in the cold, but older passengers contemplate the notion of boarding the train at the platform and seeking out their carriage by taking to the cluttered aisle and concertinaed carriage connections. Despite the fact the express will be in Te Kuiti for ten minutes, there is always anxiety. It's partly excitement of course, with passengers hellbent on getting aboard.

One of my first memories of the Auckland to Wellington Express, in the days when it still seemed as if we were on our way to a new paradise, occurred as we stood on Te Kuiti Station staring northwards willing the express to appear. In the mid-fifties trains were still a sensible way to go, particularly on a long journey — and Te Kuiti to Wellington on the main trunk was long enough. It would take us all night, basically from 7.30pm to 7.30am, and I couldn't wait to get started.

Staring northward up the track it was possible to see the headlights of the approaching express from a couple of kilometres away. Up there, just beyond Railway Town, the line came in on a curve around the flank of a hill, and just before the river bridge the lights pulsated suddenly. After staring fixedly for fifteen minutes, imagining car headlights from the adjacent road and reflections off metal surfaces as the sun went down behind Ben Lomond Hill to be the approaching train, the sudden bright glare, like another sun coming up, sent a shot of adrenaline through my veins.

You couldn't hear anything initially, but when a long blast of steam from the engine's whistle hung in the cool air, seconds before the banshee wail reached our pricked ears, there was no doubting that this was the approaching express. Of course it could have been an out-of-sequence goods train which would have meant the express was running late, but our father had assured us our train was running on time.

Our train. We felt extremely important at the announcement. The headlight glare grew brighter and brighter. Now you could hear the swish and sway of carriages and the decelerating chuffs of the engine. The whistle sounded shrilly at the Ward and King Street crossings where mere cars and trucks were obliged to dip their hats to the majestic express.

Our train. To think we were actually travelling on something we usually admired from a distance, or from the Te Kuiti platform on a Friday evening when our parents took us to ogle at the big black KAs or JAs and the sleek, red, steel carriages. The trains were always full and the refreshment room stampedes were real. There was little indication to us kids that the railways had already begun their downhill slide as motorcars and buses gained ground. For a time — in the mid 1950s — it seemed a balance had been struck. Even as more families became car owners the trains and railcars still provided a valid means of mass transport. Dads didn't have to drive; kids didn't have to get sick in the back of the Morris Eight on the winding, often gravel roads and mums didn't have to fuss around cleaning up messes. Trains travelled imperiously through the landscape. They might swish and sway and coal smoke was always a problem until the diesels came along, but they continued to be comfortable and basically steady. I never heard of anyone getting train sick, although no doubt it happened.

I had always respected the K-class steam engines. They were the workhorses of the main trunk and the Auckland to Wellington Express. Ks, with their recessed headlights, were fat and bulbous, no-nonsense pushers and shovers and pullers. They reflected New Zealand society at the time, when common sense and practicality were catchcries — a time when a world war was won and a depression overcome. The KAs, a later development, presented a headlight set at a more rakish, forward protrusion, which made them more appealing to us young train watchers. It was a bit like soldiers and schoolboys wearing their hats and caps at gravity-defying aspects — about as authority-provoking as you could be back then.

The Js and JAs were the other major steam engine class that hauled the express during these years. They were powerful too, but altogether sleeker — gaunt in fact, if the Ks had always been your favourite. I preferred the Js and JAs. They were a bit more exclusive; it wasn't every night you saw them pulling the expresses and limiteds. Not only were the Js and the JAs less bulbous and solid-looking than the Ks, they had always featured a forward-prodding headlight, which made them look faster. Certainly their headlights always arrived before those of the Ks.

As 'our train' clanked into Te Kuiti station, that was no K or KA at the work face — that was JA1284. I was overcome with boyish delight. More so when a second JA (I forgot to check its number) was also along for the ride. Normally the smaller AB shunter engine assigned to the Te Kuiti yard would be used, if required, for banking purposes as the express tackled the Waitete bank to the south. Our train, a longish service, already had its 'banker' assigned. And those who had worried about the awkward climb from the shingle to the carriage steps were placated when the engines disconnected from the train before seeking out the water vat.

We sidestepped the hungry hordes on their way to the refreshment rooms and clambered aboard. A slurring, stumbling old man who was 'the worse for the whisky', according to my mother, played a merry dance with us in the carriage vestibule but soon we found our seats.

In earlier times the Auckland to Wellington Express was a conduit for grog and many travellers were similarly affected. Despite on-board knowledge of the 'dry' situation imposed on the King Country, guards and other officials tended to turn a blind eye. Indeed, it was reported that one particular guard sported only one eye, the other having been lost somewhere in Flanders. It was a challenge for him to train one good eye on passengers' tickets.

Other officials were more vigilant. Writer W. L. Rapley recalls one such specimen.

> 'No liquor on the train' was one of the rules strictly enforced by honest Joe Vickers, one of the most mild and inoffensive men it would be possible to meet. He was guard, porter, shunter and general custodian of the whole passenger service.
>
> Now Joe had a particular eye for suspicious-looking bags or boxes surreptitiously piled into the van as baggage. 'He could smell it inside of a steel box,' a passenger once remarked when caught with the forbidden goods, and when requested to open up the parcel, 'because you know mister the train can't start with liquor aboard,' the passenger had no option but to acquiesce in so gentle an admonition.[2]

Doug Hutchins, my late father, recalled some of the half-hearted alcohol control measures. 'There were kegs of beer in the goods van. Everyone could see that. And wooden containers housing whisky bottles. Not so many could see that, but the guard and his minions must have known. Often the list of the train, the swaying along the Rukuhia Straights, caused spillage. Whisky seeped across the goods van or guard's van floor. Yet the officials, obviously aware of the resultant alcohol fumes, turned a blind nose — or should that be blocked? The thing was, a lot of New Zealanders despised temperance and prohibition. The King Country was a thirsty backwater. It was never a dry area simply because a bunch of wowsers said it should be so. In fact, there was more heavy drinking in the King Country because of the wowsers.'

In 1955 my father was still on the platform as the express prepared to depart. At times like this I felt uneasy about Dad's bravado. But that's what happened when they came back from the war, my mother said. They missed the sense of danger. So Dad, in peacetime, put in a late sprint across the platform and a leap at the vestibule door as the train started moving. He'd got his shot of adrenaline, a bit like the times he'd bucked the odds in the Solomon Islands where air force pilots like him pitted themselves against malfunctioning Catalina flying boats, house-sized waves and shark-infested waters, to save ditched American airmen. So my father, at Te Kuiti station, pitted himself against forward momentum, desultory loudspeaker warnings and the bidding of friends from the RSA to get on board.

As the train gathered pace Dad surfaced, his adrenaline spent, in our peacetime carriage enclosure. My mother, sister and I were glad to see him. We all hunkered down for the night as the train fought for traction up the Waitete bank. As the lights dimmed, I saw my father's profile flicker into view as the express swung through Kopaki. I tried to imagine what it must have been like out over the tropical seas of the Solomons where Dad, after a 12-hour reconnaissance flight, caught up on 40 winks. A few kilometres on at Mangapehi he was dead to the world.

It was hard for young kids to get to sleep, despite the presence of an NZR pillow or the extra bedding mothers brought with them. The foreignness of sleeping arrangements and the sheer excitement of travelling on a train you had long admired from afar kept you primed. But the steam-heating provided snug warmth and the regular sounds and movements of the train lulled you into a kind of dreamland, somewhere up on the high plateau.

Travellers who were more serious about getting some real sleep booked a berth in the sleeper carriage. The Auckland to Wellington Express was the first train in New Zealand to provide the luxury of a fold-down bed. The first such carriages contained 20 beds in six compartments and later developments saw 18 berths in seven compartments become the norm. Four-berth compartments didn't really catch on with long-distance passengers. It wasn't so bad if a family of four bunked down, but if you had to share a constricting space with complete strangers in the dead of night, the imagination could do strange things.

In 1925, two-berth cabins became standard. They were the height of comfort at the time and in 1925-1926 went on display at the Dunedin and South Seas Exhibition. A year later another batch of sleeping cars represented the apex of sophistication, this time with kitchenettes included. These were the first sleeping cars to feature steel sheathing and curved body sides. The added comfort and sleekness made for some memorable journeys in the two-berth configurations.

'WFI', writing in the *New Zealand Railways Magazine*, mentioned the time he travelled, unexpectedly, with Vincent Lopez, a world-famous wrestler. Sharing a compartment with such a 'tough guy' might have been intimidating for some, but WFI found his company riveting. Sleep was of secondary importance as Lopez spoke at length, not of wrestling, but of his time as a big game hunter in the jungles of South America and Mexico. He described in detail the habits of a particular insect that injected humans with a stupefying venom, which caused a blister to erupt on the skin. If the blister was broken by untutored fingers, blood poisoning was the upshot and death a likely outcome.[3]

Meanwhile the express was eating up the distance through a hinterland devoid of such life-threatening nasties.

On another occasion a French engineer was WFI's sleeper-car companion. Aspects of the Eiffel Tower and its construction and that of the

A bit like the Eiffel Tower. The Makatote Viaduct in the early days.
HCL-8865

Maginot Line filled the hours as the train headed through the 'viaduct country', with comparisons made with viaducts like the Makatote. International goodwill engendered by sport, and its role in breaking down barriers and wartime bitterness, became a secondary theme.

Then there was WFI's encounter with a stipendiary magistrate who, rather than produce a stern, accusatory front, proved to be as friendly as the man in the street (or the second-class carriage). He spoke fondly of the warmth of people living in isolated districts of New Zealand, where they provided him with hospitality and courtesy as he went about his often unpopular business. Some of those isolated districts and settlements signalled their presence as station lights leaked through the gaps in the window curtains. Ongarue, Okahukura Junction, Taumarunui . . .

Even more remarkable for WFI was the worn-out travelling companion who caught the train in Auckland with the intention of attending a business conference in Palmerston North. He had already travelled from the far north on the Opua Express and wished to retire early. Both travellers slept soundly through the heartland. There were no conversations about the Eiffel Tower, friendly Kiwis or vicious insects. They travelled over six hundred kilometres together and, apart from the handful of words exchanged at the outset, the journey was completed in silence — and sleep. So much for those who claimed a good night's sleep was impossible on the train.

Taumarunui. If any railway town embodied the true character of the passage of the Auckland to Wellington Express — and the train itself — it was the bustling King Country refreshment stop encountered some time after 9pm. After the long haul through the dark recesses beyond Te Kuiti, the town and its lights presented as an oasis. It seemed as if the express was entering a massive glow-worm grotto with house lights winking down from hillside streets. Passengers rubbed their eyes. Appetites stirred. The prospect of a pie and cuppa appealed to those night-owls who anticipated a long night ahead. Writer Lawrence Constable in *Home Territory* recalls his arrival at the oasis:

> In the open carriage doors the hungry and thirsty stood ready for the rush to refresh themselves as soon as the train had stopped. A sepulchral voice opened up on the loud speaker system: 'This is Taumarunui,' it intoned, with stress on every syllable. 'This is Taumarunui.' What was Taumarunui? For twelve years I had been seeing it only as a name going by in the night, a place like Taihape or Ohakune, a deserted village beside the railway line. And for just so many years I had been curious.[4]

During the heyday of the express, most New Zealanders who travelled by train had come to know Taumarunui by night. Indeed, to many, the town was nocturnal, a bustling railway stop, a netherworld, where massive K and KA engines clanked around the yard like great black monsters in a blacker night. Later, sleeker J and JA engines joined the herd. Engines on the express were changed here — KAs that had worked the expresses all the way from Paekakariki holed up in Taumarunui until southbound trains arrived, while JAs that operated from Taumarunui to Auckland built up steam in the shadows. The smaller J class, often deployed to haul trains along the Okahukura to Stratford branch, and on to New Plymouth, jostled for line space.

For engine watchers, Taumarunui was a version of paradise, quite likely to create a diversion from the serious business of topping up with refreshments. Parallel worlds operated side by side. As hundreds of strangers to the town queued at the refreshment rooms, an establishment that was to be made famous by Peter Cape's New Zealand folk song 'Taumarunui (on the main trunk line)' a couple of years later, the people of Taumarunui were concluding their Friday night gambols in the main street. Friday night shopping was winding down, even as young folk hovered and yahooed on street corners, or sped and skidded in beat-up old cars, before hunkering down in milk bars and jukebox joints. Half-time at the movies produced another swarm of locals who, prior to watching the feature film, *3.10 to Yuma*, about a cowboy heist on an old American train, wandered over the

An important railway town, Taumarunui was a train-watcher's paradise.

J.A.T. Terry Photo

road to see the real New Zealand version. Some looked mesmerised by the bright lights, others just looked tired after a long week.

Taumarunui railway staff and local volunteers had to look lively though, in 1940, when serious flooding disrupted the passage of the Auckland to Wellington Express. There were five passenger trains in the Taumarunui yards and over 2000 travellers swelled the local population. It was a massive exercise to feed and transport the exodus as passengers were bussed, trucked and taxied the 20 or so kilometres beyond the flood damage to board trains dispatched from the south.

The incident alerted the nation to the prominence of Taumarunui as a railway nerve centre. New Zealanders learned that this was where '30 to 40 engines of all types came for a Sunday rest'. W. Hearn Thomas, writing in the *New Zealand Railways Magazine* went on to embellish the railway atmosphere of the town.

> It is here, too, where the big express engines are changed while passengers are resting their heads on pillows oblivious of the safety-first work that is being done on their behalf. All they know of it is the music of the tapper as he goes his round tapping the wheels, and the steaming of the engines past their windows before the gentle bump tells them the train is ready once more to carry them into the dark of the night like passengers in the Ghost Train.[5]

Taumarunui was now a far cry from the days in the 1900s when only one passenger train departed from the station at 6.50am. Every day, except Sunday, it headed out for Frankton Junction, and when it returned to Taumarunui at 8.10 in the evening, it became the event of the day. Most of the townsfolk flocked to the station to welcome the train, thereby setting off a trend that lasted for years. One local businessman developed such a reputation for meeting every train he was nicknamed 'Pelorus Jack'.

According to the 1955 timetable the express was due to depart Taumarunui at 9.16 but no one worried about such niceties now that we were in the grip of the train's will. And that included time — and weather, if you inclined to the view that Taumarunui's rain was often triggered by the massive steam clouds given off by all those engines. It would be all of four hours before we pulled into the next refreshment stop at Taihape. Some hoped to sleep through that prospect. Others, more realistic, angled for another pie. And angled their bodies across seats, armrests and windowsills, the better to find comfort and snatches of slumber. Carriage lights went out, just as they did back in 1920, when Auckland-born writer H. Hector Bolitho travelled across the same stretch.

> There was a hearty farewell, and then the party settled down to the long journey through the rainy night. The clouds parted frequently, permitting the moon to illuminate lonely farmhouses, long white country roads and groups of darkling pines.[6]

Bolitho went on to become an established writer of non-fiction in Britain. The Auckland to Wellington express went on to climb the escarpment up to the central plateau, after swinging and climbing through the curves of Piriaka, Kakahi, Owhango and Oio. The rain stopped, although there was no sign of the moon.

I wanted to be able to tell my mates I stayed awake throughout the journey; that I had been there, consciously, when the train creaked and groaned up the Raurimu Spiral, when it roared across the viaducts and opened out along the high plains around Waiouru.

Peter McCaughan, a Hamilton historian, recalls the time he and a contingent of compulsory military trainees, captivated by their first sight of snow, jumped out into the moonlight and indulged in a snow fight, as the train waited somewhere to cross another train. Going from the toasty warmth of the steam-heated carriage

What goes round must go up or down. A poster extolling the wonders of the world-famous Raurimu Spiral.

ATL-Eph-B-RAIL-1930-01

to the bitterly cold outdoors was initially a shock to the system, but soon the heat generated by a gaggle of high-spirited young men running round like panicked sheep as the snowballs flew, compensated. When they returned to the carriage their clothes were saturated. Snow was, after all, just frozen moisture, and a good deal of uncontrollable shivering set in, despite the warmth of the carriage.

I slept through National Park, Waiouru and its army base. I was hoping to see the flanks of Ruapehu wreathed in snow, but that night a heavy cloud cover denied any moonlight, I was told, so even if I had managed to stay awake there would have been little to see, save a group of hardy souls alighting at National Park Station, where they joined road connections to the Chateau Tongariro for a weekend's skiing. And at Waiouru, the highest station on the main trunk, there would probably have been a bunch of nervous CMTs (Compulsory Military Trainees) leaving the train to undertake a less glamorous sojourn.

The Auckland to Wellington Express had a reputation as the train that carried thousands of travellers through some of New Zealand's most dramatic country. And yet, if you were awake and aware, you couldn't see it. Clear moonlit nights provided some compensation, and the bright station lights and the arcing glow of the engine's headlight. Outlines of mountains, shadowy farmhouses and barns and ghostly bush stands prevailed when the moon was high, but often the cloud cover produced a mantle of impenetrable darkness.

The rhythm of the train continued to lull passengers into a twilight zone. Dreams of days gone by floated to the surface, as images of the express from its earliest days entered the mix.

> It was with some hilarity that we bade farewell to our friends at 2am in the morning at Te Kuiti and entered the crowded train. We were in holiday mood. We sat where we could. John and I in the same seat and Rowley beside a kindly stranger on whose shoulder he lay fast asleep when daylight came next morning. We were in a second class carriage. The Christmas spirit was already abroad. At Taihape a bushman in bowler

> hat and blue serge suit got in and commenced to entertain his fellow passengers. Standing up at the end of the compartment he gave us a tap dance to begin with. Then producing a bottle of whiskey he offered it to those adjacent by drawing a cork and making them drink it neat. He stood over them exhorting them to 'Tear it inter yer. Tear it inter yer. Tear it inter yer.' After which he had one himself and gave us a song. We were at the other end of the carriage, however, and sitting quiet were not compelled to participate in his generosity.[7]

Spencer Westmacott described the above encounter with the old express in his book, *The After Breakfast Cigar — Selected Memoirs of a King Country Settler*. Things were altogether more decorous — or appeared to be — when author Roy Sinclair in his book, *Rail — The Great New Zealand Adventure*, related the story of a well-mannered young lady who was allocated an aisle seat next to a well-enough presented young man. The latter, on the long, overnight journey, had recourse to the carriage window and surrounds on which to rest his head when sleep overcame him. Not so the aloof young madam who, despite friendly overtures from the man, attempted to keep her distance physically and verbally. Attempts to sleep bolt upright failed (there were no surfaces on which she could lay her pretty little head) and when the young man roused he found the standoffish young lady sleeping with her head on his shoulder.[8]

As they left the train at the end of the journey the young man reminded the girl that, although there had been no formal introductions between the two, they had in fact slept together. Extreme embarrassment washed over the woman. Nothing happened, as they say, but there were other instances when proximity and opportunity led to risqué behaviour. The darkness of tunnels, the bleak night itself, and the concealment provided by blankets and coats, saw the explosion of passions and dramatic outcomes. Strangers occasionally became more than friends. Some travellers met their lifelong partners and swore fealty to one another before the train reached Wellington.

Eruptions of another kind visited the path of the Auckland to Wellington Express in 1954, when Mount Ngauruhoe blew its top. Passengers recall seeing the fiery glow from the train as if the mountain was only a kilometre or two beyond the tracks. Others, like the whiskey tippler from Taihape, many years ago, might have put it down to a swig too many.

In 1955 the mountain's light show has long since run its course as passengers prepare for the 1.30am refreshment stop at Taihape. Some make enquiries regarding the whereabouts of the Tangiwai Bridge, scene of New Zealand's worst rail disaster, just two years previously. We passed that horrifying point many kilometres ago, before Waiouru. Had anyone been able to see the Whangaehu River, which, engorged with a lahar from the Mount Ruapehu crater lake, caused the disaster in 1953, they would have been nonplussed by its insignificance.

Taihape, well on the wrong side of midnight, produces the now familiar gallop to the refreshment room. My father, having slept through Taumarunui, leads the charge. The same speed and guile that made him a prominent wing three-quarter in rugby, means we have our supplies of refreshments before many others. It's probably just as well, as the train only

Tangiwai Station five years before the Tangiwai disaster. The nearby Whangaehu stream turned into a destructive force in 1953.

J.A.T. Terry Photo

stops for eight minutes, rather than the usual ten, and seems impatient to be on its way.

It's essentially all downhill from here, as we head into the escarpment country dominated by the Rangitikei River. The line around Mangaweka is notably curved and cramped with steep gradients and several tunnels, and the massive Mangaweka Viaduct seems to leave the train suspended as it crosses a virtual valley.

Marton Junction, where the New Plymouth line meets the main trunk, sees the train change direction from southwesterly to southeasterly, as it heads across the Manawatu Plains. Halcombe, Feilding and Bunnythorpe ghost past in the night, before Palmerston North emerges from the shadows.

Sir Joseph Ward, a political prevaricator, whose actions – or lack of them – meant the Express still travelled through the heart of Palmerston North in 1955.

ATL-B-094-025

In 1955 the train still runs through the middle of town, and the town fathers are still annoyed by the fact. As long ago as 1925 construction had begun on the Milson Deviation, a development that would solve the problem of noisy trains and congestion in the heart of Palmerston North. The new line was designed to carry the train around the outskirts to the west. A lack of government funds postponed work on the deviation in 1928, the year the United Party and its less than hearty Prime Minister, Sir Joseph Ward, were elected to office. Further political expediencies intruded after Labour was swept into power in 1935, and after work recommenced in 1938, the outbreak of World War II led to further delays. It wasn't until the 1950s that the project saw further progress made.

During the war, while travelling through Palmerston North, Dad and his buddies used to take advantage of the ten-minute refreshment stop and hightail it across the road to the Café de Paris, an exotic sounding pub near the square. At 4.30 in the morning there was little chance of Dad replicating the mad dash associated with troop trains and specials of the war years. Besides, he was in the middle of another 40 winks.

He may have been dreaming of troop trains. The calamity before the storm: temporary uproariousness in an all-male domain before heading for training before going to war. Or training before training, in the sense that trains were the accepted means of shifting military personnel.

During World War II, many young Kiwis converged on Trentham Military Camp in the Hutt Valley. Several passenger lines accommodated troop trains, but the North Island main trunk was a common conduit for 'cannon fodder', as harsher critics of the war effort would have it. As a wide-eyed kid during the postwar years, when troop trains were still a prominent feature, I used to wonder about the middle-of-the-night phantom trains.

My grandmother lived within a hundred metres of the main trunk and, because of my early fascination with trains (plus the fact that my parents were pleased to see the back of me from time to time), I was occasionally allowed to stay overnight at Nana's place. During the long night I'd watch the trains heading north and south: the plodding goods trains, the early morning express, the limited, relief expresses during the holidays — and the troop trains, strange, unheralded passenger services with carriage lights pulsing through the fog. No one slept on those.

Had I been born ten years earlier, I would have had the chance to see troop trains heading for Trentham and Waiouru and the temporary camps established during the war years. I would have seen the flitting shadows of young men who never made it back from the battlefront, although as a young boy that eventuality would have been the furthest thing from my mind.

During the years of World War II, passengers on troop trains accounted for nearly one third of all New Zealand rail passenger movements. Troop trains during World War I were scarcely less significant. In 1915, Trentham Military Camp, as one example, accommodated over 8000 men.

Frances Brebner, writing in the *New Zealand Railways Magazine*, reflected the intensity of the World War I war effort — and the critical role of the railways: 'Four mixed trains conveyed a number of troops and horses to Thorndon Station one fateful Monday, three similar trains running on the Tuesday, and a further four on the Wednesday.'[9]

On the Thursday of the same week the railways ran an excursion service that carried friends and family to Wellington to attend the public farewell at Newtown Park for troops heading to the various war zones. The farewell was described as 'enthusiastic.' They were jingoistic times — the Mother Country needed support and New Zealand was only too keen to oblige.

Male bonding and bravado was all part of the process of persuading young men to go to war, to serve their king and country. Scenes on railway stations from which troop trains departed invariably presented a contrasting human face. The young men on the trains were boisterous and boyish. This was the prelude to the biggest adventure in their young lives. Why wouldn't they be waving wildly and excitedly at family and friends, as if they were off to paradise? Meanwhile the faces on the platform were uniformly grim, even those of the children.

The local brass band played. Older men — fathers and uncles — doffed their hats. Some women, particularly the girlfriends, wept quietly. Despite it's name, World War I was not the world's first war. Older folk remembered the agony of loss, the downside of the big adventure. But the bullet-proof young men of New Zealand — Britain's most generous colony in terms of human sacrifice — often leered up on overcrowded troop trains, drinking alcohol, smashing and discarding crockery and making life difficult for refreshment room attendants.

Age would not weary many of them; family and friends sensed that as the band played on and men continued to doff hats, and women shed a tear, now that the troop train was just a smudge on the horizon, loops of coal-smoke from the engine hanging in the air as an early memorial to those who would never make the return journey.

There was nothing great about the Great War. It dragged on for five years and nearly 17,000 New Zealanders lost their lives. The debacle of Gallipoli, where 2721 Kiwis died, hit New Zealand hard. And yet, here we were, little more than twenty years on, waving farewell to another generation of young men, off to fight in another World War. The Great War was supposed to signal the end of such all-consuming conflicts, but no one managed to convince Hitler, Mussolini, the Japanese and other nasties.

The departure of World War II troop trains was often attended with less ballyhoo.

World War II accounted for another 11,625 Kiwi lives. As casualty figures became apparent, troop trains developed an ominous aspect. Perhaps that's why my father and his mates slipped away for a beer at Palmerston North. The alcohol was becoming more consoling than celebratory. And good old rugby was another diversion.

Jim Henderson, in the *Official History of New Zealand in the Second World War, 1939 — 1945*, cites the recollections of Paul Donoghue, a young New Zealander off to war:

> The 11th of January 1940 was the last day in civilian life for some 800 members of the original 22nd Battalion, and like many another that day I had to decide just what gear to take to camp with me, and it seemed perfectly natural to include football boots, socks, pants and jersey in the equipment. The next morning saw us off to Trentham . . .[10]

Fifteen years later, in 1955, the peacetime special — the Auckland to Wellington Express, pulled out of Palmerston North.

Manawatu merged into Horowhenua. The express was really going for it now, along the friendlier grades between the Tararua Ranges and the Tasman Sea. Shannon, Levin, Manakau, Otaki. The line was getting closer to the ocean with each passing station. Some considered Paraparaumu the beginning of the Wellington city conurbation, but to most it was just another whistle-stop in the middle of night and nowhere.

Paekakariki represented a whole lot more. In 1940 electrification of the line from here to Wellington was completed and the station became the southernmost extent of steam engines. From Paekakariki electric engines (EW class) took over. Because of the time it took to exchange our faithful steam engines for the altogether blander electric, it was deemed appropriate to slot in one more refreshment stop.

Wellington was only 40 odd kilometres away. We were running a bit late. Beyond Paekakariki the line hugged the Kapiti Coast, and the sight

The end of the line for steam. An electric engine, like this EW, picked up the reins at Paekakariki and drew the Express to journey's end.
D.R. Simpson

of the Tasman Sea glinting as the first light of dawn peeked through was enough to render you wide awake. Despite the broken sleep and length of travel, it was a magical moment. Wellington was just around the corner — or the one after that. Then the line left the sea and hopes were dashed, but soon, beyond Plimmerton, the more settled waters of Porirua Harbour deceived some travellers, including me, into thinking we had reached Wellington Harbour.

The sea disappeared again and we were threading suburban valleys, where lights were going on in commuter kitchens, briefcases loaded with lunches, and umbrellas, coats and hats taken down from hall racks. Suddenly the lights disappeared and we were in the first of the two long Tawa Deviation tunnels. We had heard about the tunnels, built to facilitate passage into Wellington. Before that, trains had to clamber up and down the steep line between Johnsonville and the city. Our grandmother used to tell us how the old line demanded an extra, banking engine just to get up the hill through the lofty suburbs to the north. So they built the Tawa Deviation and our train had nothing more to do than go straight through two holes in the hills.

Nana said the tunnels were long, but the first went on forever. It was 4323 metres, and at one stage we thought we were on our way to the South Island through another tunnel our grandmother hadn't told us about. Tiredness, having turned to wide awakeness, now plunged into panic. Eventually there was light at the end of the tunnel, but it was only predawn gloom and then only for as long as it took the express to cross the bridge over the Ngauranga Gorge road. Then we were in another tunnel.

People were fussing about in the carriage now. Bags were being jostled out of luggage racks. Babies were crying. Ladies were putting on their faces. Some passengers still slept, including Dad, who had nodded off in the first tunnel. Faces reflected off the windows. I looked as if I needed a haircut, but my mother put her face on while slicking down my cowlick, caused by too much tossing and turning. My sister adjusted her ribbons. Dad roused.

With a roar the express bursts out of the tunnel and suddenly Wellington Harbour is everywhere. The sun has risen somewhere beyond Eastbourne – a reasonable assumption, because I know the sun rises in the east, which is where Eastbourne is. That's why they called it Eastbourne. It is also one of the few suburbs I know the name of, and it is where we'll be staying.

It's a partly cloudy day and you can tell by the way the line-side vegetation is swaying that Wellington's famous wind is abroad. We gather up our belongings.

> And after the new day has dawned . . . like a silver filigree woven into her dreams comes the awareness of achievement — the realisation of having travelled far — and the excitement of impending arrival.
>
> The express train reaches its destination. Our traveller alights rested, refreshed, attractive and alert (a man would also have been shaved). In her heart there is a song, for that's the way she feels . . . [11]

That's how a piece of New Zealand Railways Publicity advertising had it, although to be fair, it related more to the experience of riding in a sleeper. Nonetheless, my mother was humming contentedly as we headed down the aisle. No one had been sick, we were now firmly on holiday and the war was over.

Finally the express pulls into Wellington Station, a terminus fit for a king of trains. It wasn't always like this. Audrey B. King wrote in 1939:

> Viewing the magnificent Wellington Station the memory comes back of Te Aro Station, of the trains puffing busily through the city streets and one hesitates to think of such a thing happening today. It is difficult to believe that less than sixty years ago, the North Island Main Trunk line was merely a dream in the minds of a few citizens, and that the proposal for the construction of the railway was viewed with disfavour and doubts. Yet such was the case.[12]

In 1955 such conjecture stood for nothing. Wellington station at the end of the main trunk, the sacred divining rod of the Auckland to Wellington Express, seems as real and as immutable as the mountains back up the track on the high plateau. On the platform alighting passengers swirl. The strangers in the night now appear familiar. I catch a glimpse of a hulking man I am sure is a famous All Black. No doubt other famous faces take their place in the stream of tired, often ashen-faced survivors.

The express has always carried its fair share of celebrities and notables, from the very outset. Clara Butt, the English concert vocalist, recalled her arrival at Wellington during the course of an extensive tour of Australasia.

> One night, at 11 o'clock, we arrived, very tired at a place where we had to give a concert next day, expecting to go quietly to the hotel and get some rest. To our consternation we found the station absolutely packed with people, and a dais erected, upon which stood the Mayor and councillors, who made long speeches of welcome. The town band was also present, while a torchlight procession paraded the streets, and the hotel and Town

Hall were magnificently illuminated. The procession eventually escorted us to the hotel, which we reached just before one o'clock. In this case we were almost killed by kindness. We had a somewhat unpleasant experience at a prominent hotel in Wellington, where they refused to take us in because we were 'play-acting people'.[13]

Even 'play-acting people' travelled on the express. It was the people's conduit during the golden era of rail travel.

Dame Clara Butt, with Kennerly Rumford and Maughan Barnett, on stage at the Wellington Town Hall.

ATL-PAColl-9119-2

Our arrival is less heralded. My aunt and uncle greet us with hearty smiles and a hamper of food, although it's the wrong end of the day for a picnic. It's great to be in Wellington, although there's a certain sadness in leaving the train. Then again I wouldn't want to turn around and go all the way back the way we'd just come — not for a week or two anyway. Not like a young woman during World War II, the very small girlfriend of a soldier who hid her in the luggage rack, where she slept the night away under greatcoats and travel bags. The soldier was off to war and couldn't bear to say goodbye to his sweetheart. Station officials at Wellington were in a quandary when they discovered the stowaway. Was her plight the result of sinister actions or simple high spirits? Before the matter went any further she was put on the next train back to her King Country family, who had yet to notice she was missing.

Apparently the express was often half an hour late. Our train pulled in 40 minutes behind schedule.

'The express can't even be late on time,' my father joked in his usual dry way.

In later years I travelled on everything the main trunk route of the Auckland to Wellington Express could throw at me. The express itself was a constant companion, but the limiteds, despite their more challenging departure times from Te Kuiti, going south, had their own appeal. The first time I experienced the scenic delights denied travellers on the night trains was in 1968, when the Blue Streak railcar was introduced. Four years later the Silver Fern railcar took over, and in 1971 the old Night Limited was replaced by the all-sleeper Silver Star.

The iconic Auckland to Wellington Express was replaced by the Northerner in 1975, before it too was withdrawn. Today's Overlander service, introduced in 1991, replaced the Silver Fern railcars on the daylight runs.

Russell Young, a frequent traveller on the main trunk, recalls his first encounter with the Overlander:

> The first thing that strikes me is the quietness of the train. Most of my recollection of train travel is full of noise. Conversation has to be lowered so that the person in the seat behind does not overhear. The sedate speed is relaxing. There is time to run the eyes across to a tiny town park where once there were primary school rugby trials; time for the memories to effervesce. At the next stop we discover the observation car at the rear of the train, which will be ideal for viewing the Raurimu Spiral during the next section. We find the observation car quickly becomes a conversation car, as the seating arrangement brings you in contact with at least half a dozen fellow travellers.

The expresses, limiteds and railcars have all gone. The biggest loss for many was the Auckland to Wellington Express. Rail folk called it the 227, most called it the express, or even just 'the train'. On the Thursday prior to the Easter break in 1939, it was one of eight passenger trains that carried thousands of New Zealanders between Auckland and Wellington. Another eight travelled from the capital to the queen city. Half the country seemed to be on the move. A certain pandemonium descended but everyone got to where they wanted to be.

Carol Clark, another regular traveller, recalled the same sense of chaos when her family journeyed from Wellington to Palmerston North several years later. They couldn't find carriage X, where their tickets stipulated their allocated seats would be. In the confusion, as the train pulled out, the father jumped on anyway, while mum and the kids remained on the platform. There was always a relief express in those days, and one such configuration provided considerable relief for the stranded members of the family. Four hours later the family were reunited in Palmerston North. A bit of fur flew over the re-heated fish and chips at Carol's aunty's place, but what were four hours in the larger scheme of things?

Besides, the true domain of the Auckland to Wellington Express lay further up the track, in the darkened hills and plateaux of the central North Island. Poet and author Will Lawson, a Kiwi who went on to write several successful novels while living in Australia, summed up the unique ambience of the Auckland to Wellington Express as it passed through the middle of nowhere in the depths of night.

> There was never a light in the little town
> And a soft screen glowed from the cars,
> When we backed the Lord of the Ranges down
> In the light of the watching stars.
> Soft as the breath of a summer's breeze
> The hooks and chains were drawn;
> In the silent cars behind, at ease,
> The sleepers slumbered on.[14]

2 A prince among travellers

The royal train, 1920

King George V of England made it known at the Imperial War Conference in 1917 that his eldest son and heir to the throne, Edward, Prince of Wales, might possibly visit New Zealand at the conclusion of hostilities. That possibility became reality when Prince Edward arrived on our shores in 1920, after sailing out on Britain's largest battleship, HMS *Renown*. Patriotic New Zealanders, particularly those who were young and female, could barely control themselves. Their mothers had moments of excitement too, and the population in general set about organising a royal tour that would do New Zealand proud.

A royal train, to transport the prince through a goodly part of the Dominion was assembled, with no expense spared. It was a train fit for a soon-to-be king.

Young boys were captivated as much by the gleaming train assembled for the occasion as by the visit of the prince. W.W. Stewart, the famous New Zealand railways photographer, artist and writer was as motivated as anyone.

> As a small boy I was fascinated by the brightly coloured pictures of the English royal trains in my railway picture books, and so when in 1920 it was announced that the Prince of Wales was to visit New Zealand I was determined to get some photographs of his train.
>
> I approached the loco foreman; he said I could take what I liked as far as he was concerned, though he couldn't give a written authority. He advised me to see the locomotive engineer, which I did, only to receive exactly the same answer plus the advice that I should see the Chief Mechanical Engineer who was due soon to inspect the royal train. This I did, and the CME showed me the train personally, but in answer to my request for an authority to take pictures he said he could do nothing himself and suggested I see the senior police inspector! Undaunted, off I went again, only to receive the same answer yet again, but this time with the advice that I should see the Minister of Internal Affairs! At this point I gave up and when the royal train finally made its run I joined the many hundreds of lineside viewers.[1]

Opposite

Loyal to the Royals and scarcely a bare head in sight. Aucklanders come out to see the 1920 royal train as it departs the city.

J.A.T. Terry Collection

Prior to heading out on his tour through the Dominion, the Prince of Wales inspected the Guard, a swathe of unswerving military men, assembled on the platform. He may have inspected the other guard — the privileged railway official assigned to oversee the train — although this was not mentioned in dispatches. The pilot train, gifted with the solemn duty of drawing the ire, and possible fire, of anti-royalists and testing the track, had of course already departed. Soon after the prince's train chuffed into the suburbs, an emergency train followed with the broad brief to attend to anything untoward that may, on the slightest offchance, befall the official train.

Surprise has been expressed at the need for a pilot train, to clear the path ahead for the royal train. However, it wasn't just the perceived need to ensure the safety of the track. There were elements of New Zealand society who were by no means royalist at heart. The incidence of 'conscientious objectors' in the Great War had alerted the authorities to a minority who dissented from the majority view, and perhaps even had it in their so-called 'black hearts' to do harm. Threats of a rail strike suggested that even good working-class subjects, led by the nose by disaffected troublemakers, as the official line would have it, could be waiting to impede the royal train's progress.

After all, there had been security precedents. In 1901, when the Duke and Duchess of Cornwall and York toured, the track from Wellington to Petone along which their royal train travelled was watched over by close to 400 men, as a safety precaution.

On 27 April 1920 the royal train carrying the Prince of Wales and his retinue pulled out of Auckland Station with AB663 at its head. If you were travelling south, the only way out of town in those days was via Newmarket and Remuera, as the waterfront route wasn't completed until 1930. Thousands of well-wishers thronged the suburban stations and an almost uninterrupted line of cheering supporters filled the gaps between the station hubs.

Everyone came out of the woodwork. The Prince of Wales was as popular a drawcard as the Beatles would be in a later era. In the lee of the

Great War, he was a populist phenomenon, scion of the royal family of an empire that had prevailed against great odds. Had he been the product of hard-nosed, working-class Liverpool, a pilot-train, and another in his slipstream, may not have been necessary. But while the prince was privilege personified, even in a time when New Zealanders were almost totally smitten, there were detractors.

In Auckland, as the train prepared to depart, the occasional drunks and dissenters were swallowed up by the pomp and circumstance, the military and the mayoral, in the unabashed adulation of the boyish prince. In the shadows, the disaffected mouthed threats.

'His lot took our boys' lives,' a woman screamed, barely discernible above the clamour and brass band oompahs. New Zealand's singular sacrifice in supplying more cannon fodder for England's war than anyone else was bound to have a pernicious fallout.

Despite the doubters, the 1920 royal train was again a tremendous drawcard, as were later royal trains. Over the years six royal trains enlivened the country. As long ago as 1869 an earlier Duke of Edinburgh travelled on Christchurch's broad gauge railway. In 1901 the Duke and Duchess of Cornwall and York toured, followed in 1927 by the Duke and Duchess of York, and in 1934-1935 by the Duke of Gloucester. Finally Queen Elizabeth II and Prince Philip, the Duke of Edinburgh, utilised the last of the steam-hauled royal trains in 1953-1954, to meet and greet a besotted nation.

Royalist fervour was profound in 1920, and loyal subjects climbed on vantage points in their hundreds. It might have been thousands; it certainly seemed like it. After all, Auckland was now a city of one hundred thousand, New Zealand's largest. Rupert Brooke, the English poet, once visited Auckland and made some interesting, if sweeping observations. All the people were ugly, according to Brooke and 'very upper middle-class, no poor, and the Government owning hotels and running char-a-bancs. All the women smoke and dress very badly, and nobody drinks.'[2]

Whatever their station and personal habits, Aucklanders were out in force to farewell the prince and his train.

Soon the houses receded and bright green paddocks prevailed. At Pukekohe, the first stop, the platform was clogged with another kind of greenery — ferns and foliage — and school children. A pattern was established at the outset; everywhere the train stopped enthusiastic townsfolk greeted the prince. After all, this was the boy (he was 26 at the time) who was destined to become King of England, the country with which New Zealand's bonds were still very strong. The war had come to its conclusion little more than two years previously. Despite the terrible loss of young lives, the unflinching bond between Britain and New Zealand was strengthened. It helped of course that Britain had won. Would New Zealand be greeting the prince so vociferously if he was the flag-bearer of a defeated nation?

Through the North Waikato and towns like Huntly and Ngaruawahia the train was greeted by wildly cheering crowds, although the royal special didn't stop until it reached Hamilton, located on the slow-flowing Waikato River. Much of the route had accompanied its wide brown waters, and occasionally workers on barges and river boats could be seen waving.

The very essence of the link with England, and the military miasma of the times, was personified at Hamilton Station. There the royal party was greeted by Mr P. H. Watt, the mayor, wearing the uniform of an artillery gunner, a post he had occupied while serving in the Great War.

The train headed east out of Hamilton, across the Waikato River at Claudelands, and made for Rotorua. The lushness of the plains and evidence of prosperous dairying country was around every corner, although the train didn't encounter too many of these until it passed through Morrinsville, where heading due south it took the entourage through Kiwitahi, Walton, Waharoa, Matamata, Hinuera, Okoroire and its hot springs spa, and Putaruru.

The plains gave way to hills as the line curved eastward again and Rotorua beckoned. The steam engine had its mettle tested as the Mamaku Ranges and the settlement of Mamaku were mounted with ease, before the line descended towards Lake Rotorua, glinting through the native bush and forests.

At Rotorua Prince Edward encountered the 'great Maori welcome', a unique feature of his journey. Many Maori made the pilgrimage to Rotorua, swelling the ranks of the tangata whenua, from all points of the compass. The prince also became acquainted with another side of the railway tracks — a railway workers strike, described by commentators of the day as an 'ultra modern and popular recreation'. With Rotorua's population having swelled to three times its normal size, reliance on the railways for food and provisions, as well as ease of passage, caused anxiety. The strikers were serious in intent and even the royal personage was not spared. His train was due to leave Rotorua at three in the afternoon, but it took another nine hours before arrangements were negotiated between strike authorities and rail department boffins, and the royal train pulled out. During the night the train returned the way it had come, arriving back in Auckland in the early morning.

To see and be seen. The observation car and viewing platform of royal trains was a feature even in 1920. Here the viewing platform of the 1953 royal train attracts bystanders.

J.A.T. Terry Photo

After two days' wait in Auckland the royal party again set out for the south. On the Sunday the pilot train earned the distinction of being the only other train permitted to run on the New Zealand rail network. Close at heel was the royal train.

Prince Edward travelled in the last carriage. Accompanying him were Admiral Sir Lionel Halsey, Lieutenant-Colonel Grigg, Lord Louis Mountbatten, Sir Godfrey Thomas, Lord Claude Hamilton, Captain the Honourable Piers Leigh and other notables. The ministerial car was overseen by Sir William Fraser and Mr J. Hislop. The press carriage included amongst its distinguished English journalists, Mr Keith Murdoch of *The Times*, Mr John Sandes representing English and Australian newspapers and Mr Everard Coates of Reuters.

Mr Morgan of the Press Association, Dr Guy H. Scholefield, the Government chronicler Mr Malcolm Ross and Mr H. Hector Bolitho flew the flag for the New Zealand press.

Journalists and writers travelling on the train spoke mainly of the positive, how New Zealand roused in a collective show of unmitigated joy and respect. When someone threw a bunch of leeks into the royal car during a motorcade in one centre, little was said about the possible disaffection of Welsh New Zealanders. Instead it was simply a matter of deflecting discussion into the multitude of floral tributes and other more sensible symbolic gestures. Or contemplating the notion of the leeks finding their way into the royal stew pot that evening.

After stopping at Frankton the train reached Te Kuiti. H. Hector Bolitho wrote of the stop as being the first strictly official event along the main trunk.

> The Mayor, Mr G. P. Finlay, Captain Kennedy, D.S.O, M.C. and the schoolmaster represented citizens, soldiers and children respectively. All three disposed of their part in the cheerful proceedings, the children reinforcing the impression that New Zealand is a country with vast possibilities in its coming generation.[3]

Doug Hutchins, my father, recalled the account of an old Te Kuiti digger who was at the station that day.

> No expense was spared, although times were becoming tight. It was one of the great occasions for Te Kuiti and New Zealand. I was only a kid but I could recall the train vividly. It went through fairly late in the evening, time enough for some of the town's drunks to get tanked up. In fact someone said that even if the engine pulling the prince didn't need topping up with water at Te Kuiti, the old blokes who liked their tipple, some who had served in the Boer War, began topping up earlier than normal. The sly-groggers, despite the presence of police and other minders, did a roaring trade.

> The royal train of 1920 was almost as exciting an event as the actual opening of the main trunk line in 1908. The mayor made a speech on the station after the prince climbed down from his train. He was much smaller than we expected. Heirs to the throne were supposed to be very tall, us kids thought. But he was very friendly, although he seemed tired, with bags under his eyes. One of the other boys reckoned you could smell the whisky on his breath, but I reckon that was old Charlie, the 'dropper', who drank as much as he supplied. He was standing — swaying really — behind us. When he opened his mouth to join in the hip-hip hoorays, the cold night air became contaminated with booze fumes.
>
> But the prince wasn't upset by the few drunks. Official journals only recorded his encounters with sober citizens, immaculate uniformed officials and military types. And colourfully regaled mayors and councillors standing rigidly, certainly not swaying, in the strengthening wind on the gaily decorated platform. Bunting and native plants and ferns were everywhere and I remember the mayor becoming momentarily ensnared in the leaves of a ponga tree as he prepared himself for his speech.

The train sped on to Taumarunui, where Prince Edward met the district's oldest pioneer and a veteran of the Land Wars (referred to as the Maori Wars at the time). Under cover of darkness the train threaded a goodly stretch of the main trunk and, after transferring to the Taranaki line at Marton Junction, saw the light again as the train headed for New Plymouth. A formal greeting was held at Pukekura Park before the entourage rejoined the train.

Stratford, Hawera and Patea were stopping points before Wanganui was reached, where returned soldiers were heavily represented amongst the well-wishers. Many wore their war decorations.

At Marton, the royal train caught up with the prince, who had been driven by car from Wanganui. On the following leg to Woodville via Feilding and Palmerston North a motorist rose to the challenge of the speeding train and kept abreast for a time. Countrysiders rushed out to wave, including one unprepared royalist in bare feet and nightgown.

The royal ship HMS *Renown*, seen here in Waitemata Harbour, met up with the royal entourage at Napier. Anti-royalists beware!

ATL-1/2-016067-G

At Palmerston North, in 1920 the largest town on the main trunk, the royal train changed tack on its way to Napier, via the Manawatu Gorge. Disappointment was expressed regarding the lack of a railway line from Napier to Gisborne. After a triumphant journey through Hawke's Bay the train approached Napier Station, not long after sunset. There was still sufficient light to discern the thin column of smoke from the royal ship, HMS *Renown,* as she sailed into Napier on her way to Wellington.

The following morning, masses of supporters rushed to the station to farewell the prince. Amidst the pandemonium a woman attempted to board the train, totally unaware it was not a regular service. When told she had attempted to board the royal train she made light of it by proclaiming she was a direct descendent of the Irish Royal family.

'He's such a fine young fellow,' another woman on Napier Station was heard to say. 'Handsome too, in a pleasingly boyish way,' she added. 'He'll break hearts before too long, mark my words.'

The train made seven stops at towns along the way as it returned south. At Hastings a distinctive flag-decked motorcar was sighted — again. It had followed the train through several towns, such was the interest and fervour the presence of the Prince of Wales had generated. Following the stop at

Dannevirke the prince himself drove the train all the way to Woodville. At Woodville, five hotels served a population of 1000, most of whom gathered at the station. They had been informed that Prince Edward would be in the rear carriage, resplendent with its royal coat of arms. It was a total surprise to learn that the guest of honour could in fact be found in the engine cab, where he had piloted the train the 30-odd kilometres from Dannevirke, and was now locked in conversation with Lord Mountbatten.

Souvenir hunters attacked at Woodville, and a glass of toothpicks from the royal dining table was uplifted. Such wanton vandalism, as it was considered at the time, was extremely unwelcome.

Following the excitement of Woodville the train circled on to the Wairarapa line. Such was the clamour to see the prince, when Eketahuna missed out as a stopping option townsfolk turned sour. A public meeting was held and a resolution passed expressing 'profound disgust at the studied opposition of responsible officials to the people's loyal desire to greet their future Sovereign.' Effigies of the unpopular officials were burned in the main street of Eketahuna.[4]

The temperance movement's attempt to impose prohibition of alcohol in New Zealand briefly reared its fractious head, as the train reached the small settlement of Mauriceville. Back in 1920 the will of the wowsers had left its mark in some districts. Forced to close when Mauriceville 'went dry', the town's deserted hotel presented an image of lifelessness. The locals were lively though, and with no desire expressed on the part of the prince to stop for a quick ale or something stronger, he passed through the small dry town without incident.

The journey through the northern Wairarapa was notable for its dearth of official receptions and formal greetings. There was time for the prince to reflect and perhaps regret that plans for a few days of deer stalking in the Wairarapa had been waived because of the confounded railway strike. Instead, the prince made time for meeting and greeting the locals at the many station-stops along the rail network.

Masterton, Carterton and Featherston saw the train reverting to type and stopping to joyous receptions as the breeze sharpened. Auckland's balmy days were now a distant memory. Masterton, still in a 'dry' area, presented the sobering spectacle of former hotel bars converted into soda fountains.

Despite its 'dry' status, Masterton presented an old woman who waved a flag with one hand, and a half-empty whisky bottle with the other. Times were becoming hard. So was the liquor. If ever there was an example of what prohibition could do to certain members of the local populace, this was it. The bottle had disappeared by the time she was welcomed aboard to see the inside of the royal carriage. Along with many other fascinated loyalists she was invited to make a cursory inspection of the prince's sleeping, eating and travelling circumstances. She was seen to touch the pillows on which the young prince laid his head at night, as the train swayed and swished through the dark, lonely New Zealand countryside. Not that other women, stone cold sober, had avoided the temptations of reaching out for a touch of reflected glory, but the whisky-washed woman was the only one to make comment.

'What a lovely young man he is,' she slurred. 'More a boy perhaps. But I'd like to be here to fluff up his pillows, in all ways, when he himself was here.' The woman was ushered quickly off the train and sent scuttling beyond the platform, where she reconnected with her bottle. Or was it a fresh one?

At other times and stations, travelling press men wrote about the many rosy-cheeked children — and adults — who celebrated the arrival and despatch of the royal train. Children apart, you had to wonder about the ruddy faces. While the country as a whole was delighted with the royal presence, and felt empowered to be part of a glorious empire, there were many smitten by grog in a country battling with the bottle. More so now that the temperance movement had induced a rebellious colonial backlash.

At Carterton, the 'wet' area started and the rain cleared. Here a man, or woman, could drink alcohol in peace. Thousands of New Zealanders would relate to that, just as they could recall Featherston, beyond Carterton, where most of the country's infantry, artillery, mounted, machine-gun and specialist reinforcements for World War I were trained at the nearby camp. The train passed the now empty acres of army huts that made up the military base. Close to 8000 soldiers were based here, in various stages of readiness for conflict.

One of the most poignant moments occurred here, at odds with the sense of celebration and liberation throughout the royal train's long voyage through the Dominion. Prince Edward and his entourage became reflective while watching the remnants of the Featherston camp pass. But for the sacrifice of colonial forces like those of New Zealand, the war between Britain and Germany may not have been won. One of the reasons for the young prince travelling to the antipodes was to recognise the Kiwi sacrifice in the 1914-18 conflict. England would not forget. Not yet, anyway.

And now, at the largest former military camp in the Dominion, the train slowed as if to acknowledge the enormity of the local sacrifice. The moment was lent a certain sacredness by the gloominess of the now forsaken huts and fixtures. God knows how many youths — a generation of New Zealand manhood — had trained here, preparatory to shipping out to Gallipoli and the Dardenelles . . .

From the train it was just possible to discern another abandoned military installation — Tauherenikau — once a canvas town for unfit soldiers who received a strong dose of physical training in the interests of preparing them to better serve king and country in the Great War. Meanwhile the royal train and its pensive retinue sped across the Wairarapa Plains, a lowland marked by dry river beds in a now 'wet' region (the rain started again), with tangible memories and emotional scars left to testify to the part our young Dominion played in helping England stave off the German challenge.

The prince alighted at Featherston and the dignitaries gathered in front of the Wairarapa Club, an establishment built by the locals to provide a sanctuary for the men from the camps. While the engine exhaled impatiently at the station, he honoured the chambers where the young soldiers diverted themselves at uproarious dances called 'shilling hops' before returning to the camp and further training, or enlistment overseas.

Miss Harriet Card, the Featherston mayoress, and a genuine heroine to many soldiers through her work caring for soldiers' graves, was presented to him, before he returned, somewhat misty-eyed, to his waiting train. Night was falling, which seemed appropriate as a token of sober remembrance. The train turned towards the mountains — the Rimutakas — and the extraordinary engineering feat known as the Rimutaka Incline.

In many ways it was poor planning that the royal train did not attack the incline in broad daylight. If it had, the prince would have witnessed the intrepid spirit of New Zealand rail surveyors, purveyors and engineers, who hacked out an ambitious approach to the capital. The Rimutaka Incline was world-famous for its sheer audacity, a triple-tracked, adhesive climb over a virtual mountain range — severe hills if nothing else — into the valleys and undulations on the other side.

The train stopped at Cross Creek at the base of the climb. Night had fallen but that failed to deter railwaymen and their families from assembling noisily in the dark to welcome the prince. One old ganger, his hand around an unopened bottle of beer (he deigned to drink in the presence of royalty), reassured the prince that the rail strike had nothing to do with feelings of antagonism towards any individual — let alone the heir to the throne of England. The prince slapped the ganger on a bony shoulder, before re-boarding the train that now had a fleet of Fell engines, specialist units in rack-rail travel, aligned between the carriages.

Through the cold and dark the Fells chuffed manfully upward. Beyond the summit the sensation of an easier, downhill glide hit the tired passengers. The long day had seen eight stops and boisterous receptions on the line from Napier through Hawke's Bay and the Wairarapa and now, as the lights of Wellington grew in intensity and regularity, a stately stop at Wellington's Lambton Station — in the seat of government.

After a day of tipping his hat to small rural towns, the young heir was reminded by the thousands of Wellingtonians who greeted the train and lined his route that New Zealand was more than a collection of rural-serving towns — 'dry', 'wet' or otherwise.

The prince was greeted at Government House and the following day a

formal, civic reception was held at the Town Hall. The latter was described as the 'most ceremonious moment of the tour' and was followed by luncheon at the old Parliamentary Buildings. During his time in Wellington he also attended a military parade at Newtown Park, a children's day in the city's heart, a rugby match, a New Zealand historical pageant at Petone and visited the Trentham military hospital.

How we won the war. The prince reviewing the guard of honour in Wellington.

ATL-PAColl-0037-12-36

After spending several days in the capital, the prince sailed across Cook Strait to Picton, before travelling on to Blenheim and Nelson by car. At Nelson he took to the tracks again on the isolated Nelson railway. The local royal train was made up of two carriages and a van. As could be expected, the interiors were meticulously renovated and the first-class seats in the royal car were replaced with wicker chairs and small tables. Carpet, curtains and cushions were done out in blue — royal blue. Ferns, flags and shrubs on the exterior completed the decorations.

Prince Edward stood on the rear platform of the last carriage, waving to the crowds who gathered to wish him well. He had expressed the wish to see as many children as possible, and was placated by the arrival of a special

A proud day for Nelsonians and their railway. The prince waves from the royal train as it departs Nelson.

ATL-1/2-035441-G

train from Belgrove, which picked up excited kids along the rural route, all the way to Nelson city, where they joined in the mass farewell.

Although the royal train didn't stop at settlements between Nelson and Belgrove, locals flocked to see the train and its 'precious cargo'. At Richmond, 2000 people gathered, and at Glenhope, a tiny place at the end of the line, in excess of 200 people turned out.

To get to the West Coast the prince was obliged to travel by car, via Reefton to Westport. After returning by car from Westport another royal train beckoned, and soon the royal party was off through Greymouth, all the way to Hokitika. Like the lonely outposts in the Nelson hinterland they had recently travelled through, Hokitika had a strong association with gold mining and gold rushes. In 1886, as a result of gold discoveries, Hokitika boasted a population of 50,000 and numerous public houses.

The next step in the journey saw the royal train travel north along the West Coast line to Greymouth, a city with 45 sawmills in the vicinity. Beyond

Greymouth the mountains beckoned. In those days the Otira Tunnel had yet to be riven through the Southern Alps, and the train terminated at Otira, up in the foothills. The tunnel, when it was opened in 1923, became the longest in the British Empire.

After a winding, precipitous journey by coach and a contrasting easy carriage across the western reaches of the Canterbury Plains, the entourage reached Christchurch. Prince Edward was declared a Freeman of the city of Christchurch, the first person to receive such an honour in a New Zealand metropolis. A public reception was held in Latimer Square and the honoured guest was later driven through the crowded streets on his way to visit Hagley Park. He later met soldiers and children, attended a civic ball, had a flutter on the horses at the Riccarton races and attended a church service at Christchurch Cathedral. Towards the end of his three days in Christchurch he visited Christ's College and the local hospital.

From Christchurch the train headed south towards Dunedin, the Edinburgh of the south. Stops were made at Ashburton, Temuka and Timaru, the latter seeing the line emerge at the coast, after travelling for many kilometres across the broad Canterbury Plains. A few kilometres out of Oamaru the train stopped for the prince to visit Waitaki School.

From Oamaru Station the train headed into the gloom of night before bonfires lit to welcome the prince blazed away beside the tracks. At Port Chalmers, at the approaches to the city of Dunedin, hundreds of red flames highlighted the many well-wishers who came out into the chilly night.

By now the royal train had become a familiar, if temporary, adjunct to New Zealand life. Familiarity may have bred a certain ho-hum resignation on the final leg between Dunedin and Invercargill, but it certainly did not breed contempt. The prince must have been on the verge of exhaustion as flurries of ruddy, cheerful faces and snow flecked the line-side. Milton, Balclutha, Gore and Invercargill came and went before the train returned to Christchurch.

The royal train had also developed its own mystique and prestige. At Balclutha even the gentlemen of the press were bathed in reflected glory as fans thrust their autograph books in their direction. The Prince of Wales had won over all but the most cynical and hidebound.

And let us not forget the royal train itself. It had been operated with telling excellence. Mr G. McVilley, General Manager for Railways, was commended for the way he had superintended the principal means of the prince's conveyance through the Dominion.

'It's a pity we can't all have our own train like the prince,' Bill, a railway workman, said as he cleared up at the end of the day.

'With bunting and the like on the front,' replied his mate Tom, opening a beer.

'And on the sides', Bill said, making sure the shed door was locked.

'A specially polished loco.' Tom was getting wistful now.

'And our own personal toothpicks in the dining car . . .'

Even as the Prince of Wales sailed homeward out of Lyttelton Harbour, his train was stripped of its affectations for regular use on New Zealand Railways. Wrote H. Hector Bolitho:

> The train is a royal train no longer. Our bunting is folded and the blaze of electric lights has given place to the utilitarian display of ordinary times. A farewell message has been recorded in the newspapers and we know that the guest of a month has passed across the sea to further triumph. But we know that a new sense of awe and country-love has come to us and that we have a firm reason for our allegiance to the parent England. That reason is sanctified by our service in war and glorified by the knowledge that the prince is fit heir to the throne and fit symbol of the freedom for which we fought.[5]

3 Last stop, Bay of Islands

The Opua Express, 1946

In June 1976 the section of line between Whangarei and Opua finally closed to passenger traffic. The final link in the old route of the Opua Express had gone.

Back in 1975 we had attempted to travel the length of the Auckland — Opua line. It was easy enough to catch an Auckland to Helensville suburban train, where we spent the night. Helensville, which sits on the Kaipara River where it becomes estuarine, with the broad expanse of Kaipara Harbour beckoning, was a quiet but friendly backwater. Unfortunately the hotel proprietor told us the mixed goods train, which used to run between Helensville and Wellsford, stopped operating on 30 March, just a month before. We would have to get the bus to Wellsford in the morning, and Highway 16, or its equivalent back then, didn't follow the rail's passage.

From Wellsford a mixed goods train used to creak northwards through Maungaturoto, beyond Waiotira Junction and the connection with Dargaville, all the way to Whangarei, but by the time we arrived for our grand reconnoitre around Northland by mixed trains, the service was long gone. This time it wasn't a matter of missing the train by a month; it had been eight years since the closure of the Wellsford to Maungaturoto service. Luckily the mixed trains between Maungaturoto and Whangarei, and Whangarei and Opua were still running, and after resorting to buses we finally made it to the end of the line at Opua.

Ten years earlier I had travelled on the Northland railcar, a service that replaced the Opua Express in 1956, as far as Waiotira Junction. A connecting mixed train along the Dargaville branch carried me on to Dargaville, where I stayed with family friends for a few days. So in reality I had covered the entire route of the old Opua Express, although it had been in piecemeal fashion.

The trip along the Dargaville branch was memorable. Waiotira Junction itself was a lonely dot on the map, with a handful of old wooden houses and little more. The station looked important, though, with island platforms

Previous page
Paradise regained, post-World War Two. A mother and child, dressed for summer, meet the Opua Express as it completes its journey beside the Bay of Islands.
ATL-WA-30073-F

and signs that read 'Waiotira. Change here for Dargaville'. So I did — to a diesel-drawn mixed goods train that, if I recall, had little in the way of goods to carry. It looked more like a short suburban service with carriage and a guard's van behind the diesel. The Dargaville connection looked as if it would be a doddle, with only 60-odd kilometres to the terminus on the banks of the Northern Wairoa River. Such a light train would be able to pick up speed and maintain a fast run.

Wrong. The trip down the branch seemed to take forever. The train dawdled as it headed west through Pikiwahine and Tangowahine. Even back then I knew wahine was Maori for woman, and for much of the journey it seemed appropriate, as the only other passengers in the carriage on that drizzly, midweek day were two middle-aged women who talked incessantly. The train screeched and graunched incessantly too, which made it difficult to make out just what the women had so much to talk about.

Before 1941 the branch petered out at Tangowahine; at least the line in 1965 ran all the way to Dargaville. That was excuse enough for me to tango with the wahines in the all but deserted carriage, and besides, there were sound enough reasons for the train's tardiness. Much of the track was built on reclaimed peat swamp and the often yielding mudbanks of the Northern Wairoa River.

And anyway, there have been compensating features right from the outset. No sooner had the train curved away from the main line than we were negotiating the 355 m Waiotira Tunnel. A seemingly inconsequential spur, like the one to Dargaville, always attracts a certain respectability if it features a tunnel or two, and a second tunnel, the 598 m Omana Tunnel, adds that respectability. Bridges are good too, and between the junction and Dargaville there are 26 of them.

Halfway along the route the Northern Wairoa River makes its first appearance. Near Tangowahine the river loops through the landscape on its way to the sea. The line follows the river as it all but curves back on itself. Peter McCaughan, a Hamilton historian and former Northland resident, describes the river as the only one in New Zealand to flow upside down, such is its muddy appearance. As rivers go it is an impressive expanse, although beyond Te Wharau it flows away from the line which completes its course with an elaborate curve of its own, before ending at Dargaville. The women are still talking as they leave the train, although they lower their voices when they realise they have been sharing the carriage with another traveller.

Noted author Robin Hyde wrote about Dargaville, which was accessible by the Opua Express and served by its own branch line.

ATL-1/2-043599-F

Robin Hyde remembered Dargaville as 'a quaint main street where there were gas lamps, countless dogs, and Maori boys wearing magenta blazers plus peppermint-pink berets. Dargaville has electricity and has gone in for brick and concrete. It looks almost incongruously respectable.'[1]

In the days when the Opua Express connected with the Dargaville train the spectre of light patronage would not have been so prevalent. In fact it was a rollicking little ride, as many passengers sought passage, both north and south, on the express.

In 1925 the completion of the Northern line and the subsequent introduction of the passenger express from Auckland to the Bay of Islands, saw the opening up of the 'winterless north' to rail tourism. Just as thousands were flocking to Rotorua on the Rotorua Express, many now took the rail option to Opua. The Opua Express rapidly became the standard means of travel to the lustrous Bay of Islands.

By 1946 streamlined J engines have taken over from the ubiquitous AB. The bullet-nosed J is not everyone's cup of tea, with some prefering the pared back version. Streamlining is just an American fad they say, yet the J feels powerful as it draws the Opua Express out of the station, leaving central Auckland.

The year 1946 had a special lustre. World War II was over and New Zealand was returning to peacetime normality. There was a spring in the step of New Zealanders in general, including passengers on the Opua Express. That New Zealand had helped win the war filled Kiwis with pride,

A bullet-nosed engine like this one, J 1213, pulled the Opua Express in 1946.

J.A.T. Terry Photo

a feeling augmented by the knowledge that the horrors of conflict and threats of invasion no longer haunted them.

The war had ended the year before, and for New Zealanders, it ended twice. VE Day was celebrated uproariously in May and in August VJ Day produced further joyful scenes. People danced and sang in the streets as Union Jacks and New Zealand flags flapped triumphantly in an expression of unbridled patriotism.

They were heady days, tinged inevitably with tragedy and grief for those who had lost loved ones, and the 'golden weather' postwar years would see New Zealanders heading out to enjoy their private versions of paradise. The sense of freedom was tangible.

The Opua Express headed inland at 8.40am on the old south line. The Parnell Tunnel and the Domain presage the train's arrival at Newmarket Junction, where a good deal of shunting was required before the North Auckland section of the network officially began. After taking on board passengers at Newmarket Station, first-time travellers would have been alarmed to find the train suddenly backing up and reversing. Someone suggested a dignitary — perhaps Zane Grey, the famous American writer — had been late getting to Auckland Station. Or was it the Governor-General or the Prime Minister? Someone else commented loudly that railway officials wouldn't bother reversing all the way back to Auckland if Joe Average missed the train.

Trains heading north out of Newmarket Station after leaving the Auckland terminus were obliged to back on to a long backshunt siding, part of the Newmarket Triangle. It was an engineering curiosity, with no one bothering to construct a rail connection between the South and North Auckland lines beyond Newmarket Station. The latter could conceivably have been repositioned on the Auckland side of the junction points, but there was an issue of extreme curvature. Besides, pockets of land in that part of the city were all spoken for, so there was little room for new loops. The Newmarket Triangle siding remained the compromise position, and besides, young passengers rather warmed to the idea of the train going backwards for a short distance and climbing on the elevated backshunt.

Mount Eden Prison was a sobering sight as the train gathered speed beyond Newmarket through the western suburbs. Eden Park, where the All Blacks had played some of their most memorable rugby, was more in keeping with the mood of passengers. Earlier in 1946, the year international rugby recommenced after the outbreak of World War II, the All Blacks sealed a series against the touring Australians at Eden Park. The home side thrashed the tourists 31–8 at Dunedin in the first test, and although they couldn't repeat that domination at Eden Park, the 14–10 victory prompted the catchcry 'a win's a win'. Besides, their first test series in eight years had produced a two–nil result for the All Blacks and had seen the debuts of some of New Zealand's most famous players. Bob Scott, Johnny Smith, Ron Elvidge, Fred Allen and Has Catley all played in that pivotal series against the pesky Australians. Life in New Zealand was truly getting back to normal.

Many Aucklanders had experienced travelling on the 'Cemetery Train' — the Sunday afternoon Auckland to Henderson suburban service, which carried mourners either to funerals or to visit the graves of loved ones at Waikumete Cemetery. Rail officials called the service the 'Perfume Run' because of all the flowers passengers carried. Away back in 1886 blueprints were drawn up for special funeral trains to take passengers and coffins to

Waikumete. The coffins were to be loaded at Mount Eden and the train designated to wait until burial formalities were completed before carrying the funeral-goers back to the city.

Despite these good intentions, records leave some doubt as to whether these trains were actually deployed. Besides, hearses were the usual means of coffin conveyance and there remained the problem of the return train, having already invoked considerable downtime, being in no position to stop at the New Lynn Hotel, a popular watering hole where mourners could drown their sorrows and pay their last respects.

Signal boxes, back yards, curves and climbs punctuated the journey west through the suburbs. The preliminaries presaged the camber of New Zealand's northernmost express, as it continued through essentially rural backwaters punctuated by bush-covered hills and countless curves and testing grades, although the steepest climbs featured along the Auckland suburban route. From Newmarket to Mount Eden the gradient was 1 in 39, and 1 in 36 further along between Swanson and Waitakere. Despite this, many travellers gained the impression that the line to the far north had more curves and bumps than any other New Zealand main line.

Beyond Henderson the wooded Waitakere Ranges reminded travellers that soon the city would be behind them. As the train passed through Waitakere station the line, as if feeling the pull of the winterless north, quit its westward drift, and headed due north. At Kumeu memories of the old Kaipara – Riverhead railway were revived for passengers old enough to remember the way it linked the Waitemata Harbour to the east and the Kaipara Harbour on the west coast. When the new rail connection between Auckland and Kumeu was opened, the old line had outlived its usefulness. The link between Kumeu and Riverhead was scrapped and the rest, between Kumeu and Helensville South, incorporated into the main north line.

The train ambled on through pastures and around forests, before the immense Kaipara Harbour revealed fishing boats stranded and angled on grey mud flats, as tidal water drained from creeks and estuaries. At Helensville, first-time travellers couldn't help but compare the sweeping seascapes of the Waitemata to this puggy-rimmed west coast harbour, with its mangrove thickets and muddy approaches. Despite its status as New Zealand's largest harbour, it was comparatively shallow.

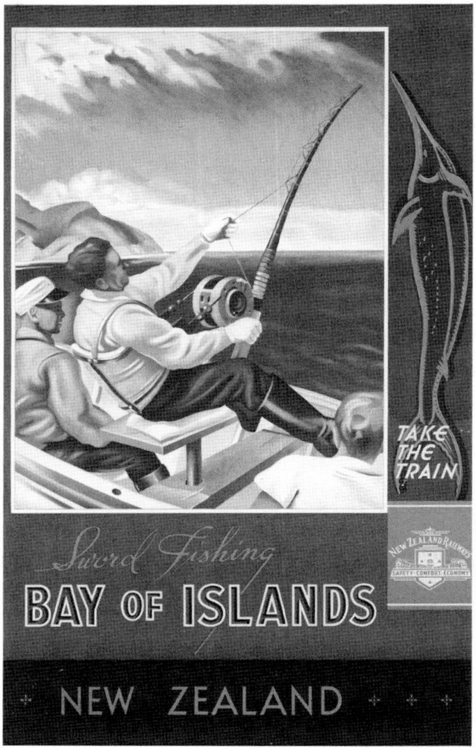

Inducement to take the train and experience the big-game fishing paradise of the Bay of Islands. A New Zealand Railways Publicity Branch poster of the 1930s.

ATL-Eph-E-RAIL-1930s-02

Zane Grey, the American novelist and big-game fisherman, must have wondered what he had let himself in for the first time he travelled to the far north by train. At low tide the Kaipara presented a patchy image; its lack of depth not exactly the setting for a deep sea big-game fisherman with dreams of snagging a marlin or two. But at least it was still our harbour, not Japan's, and in 1946 it had a charm of its own.

Helensville was a refreshment stop and as passengers became acquainted with the station and its immediate precincts the close bond between the railway and shipping became evident. Just beyond the rail yard, the Helensville wharf fringed the Kaipara River and a steamer sat in the dock. Far-flung travellers had come to town by boat to catch the train. Others left the train here to travel on the harbour to outlying settlements dotted around the Kaipara. A handful terminated their train journey to take the waters of another kind — the hot springs at nearby Parakai.

In 1913 Helensville's links with the railways and the sea had been highlighted by an event that ironically showcased the Waitemata Harbour. The battle cruiser *HMS New Zealand* visited Auckland, and hundreds of boat-watchers caught special trains from Helensville to see her, travelling through suburban stops on the northern line to the main Auckland Station. Those were still the days when mass train transit was regarded as the way to go.

From Helensville the line north followed the main road until, beyond Kaukapakapa, it struck out on its own away from the harbour. Kanohi, Makarau, Tahakeroa and Ahuroa were locations through rural Northland which, if nothing else, reminded visitors of Northland's Maori heritage. First-time visitors saw a distinctive landscape populated by mangrove swamps, thickets and nikau palms. Stands of massive kauri trees and denuded forests, along with land scarred by gum-digging, set the territory apart. Frank Sargeson, the New Zealand writer, described his journey on the Opua Express in the 1920s and touched on the various moods and features of the landscape. The unique subtropical vegetation was diverting but the broken banality of the gumlands provided an unpleasant contrast. And yet, many years later, Sargeson recalled the journey as highly memorable and pleasurable. Such is the nature of train travel, particularly when you are plying new lines and destinations.

In the early days of the line a special train known as the 'gum diggers special' carried Aucklanders north, where they were free to fossick on abandoned gum land in the vicinity of the railway. Rather than seeing this as a dead landscape, family groups collected kauri gum the diggers had left behind. These excursions were eagerly awaited and were an enriching day out in every sense, providing enough pickings to supplement a family's often pitiful income.

The Kaipara Harbour has such a massive reach that its tentacles return as the train heads northwest out of the township of Wellsford, with a fingerling estuary protruding at Te Hana. The climb up to Wellsford has been challenging, with the rail yards located on the brow of a hill, but the plunge down the other side to Te Hana and Topuni (where another Kaipara Harbour inlet appears) sees the train swinging and swaying.

A similar challenge followed beyond Topuni, with further climbing to the Ross Hill Tunnel and another roller-coaster ride down through Kaiwaka. An impressive bridge across the Otamatea 'River' carried the train, although the river was in fact another indentation of the Kaipara. The 313 m long bridge is regarded as the most notable feature on the line to the north.

The train sped up perceptibly as it left the bridge, trying for a decent run up to the grade and two more tunnels. The nearby remnants of the old Ranganui wharf are a reminder of the days when Ranganui was the line's terminus, from where cargo was shipped further afield on the Kaipara.

Maungaturoto was the next stop, where refreshments were available and the Opua Express was almost halfway to its final destination. The station and yards were surprisingly substantial, given its position, in the middle of a hilly nowhere. Engines were serviced here too, and things made more sense when you realised the major part of the town was located another six or so kilometres away, towards the Kaipara.

The train departed Maungaturoto at 12.30pm, complete with replete passengers and watered engine, as it set out for its next major stop at Waiotira Junction. Prior to that, at the lonely Taipuha siding, the north-bound train pulled over to let the south-bound express pass. Through the carriage windows the passengers seemed contented, if not downright jovial, their faces tanned. They had obviously enjoyed their time in the Bay of Islands, some perhaps a little too much — a few of the faces were sunburnt.

At Waiotira the Dargaville branch train, led by a WW class tank engine, waited for those heading towards Northland's west coast. A goodly number of passengers from Dargaville and points along the branch clambered aboard the express with a certain excitement and hopes of continuing good weather in the north.

At Portland the impressive cement works comes into sight, after the line has tended perceptibly towards the east and the prospect of Pacific Ocean views. The works operate a complex rail network of their own and at one time boasted New Zealand's largest collection of privately run steam engines. Two rail bridges carry the main line over the cement company's railway and flurries of small locos are busy working industrial trains below.

While an interesting diversion, it cannot detract from Whangarei Harbour, which now dominates the skyline. At Kioreroa, further transport relics rekindle memories. This was the site of the original port, where the old railway liftbridge used to carry trains across the harbour to Onerahi wharf.

Before the days of the Opua Express travellers from the north caught the steamer for Auckland at Onerahi.

Whangarei's spacious station provides a chance for a mid-afternoon pie and cuppa, before the engine earns its keep by tackling the long, ascending embankment away from the station. Suburban Whangarei recedes as the train continues to climb. The hammering of the engine is so insistent you fear for the sleep of those living close to the line; surely the clamour of night trains would have driven them from their beds?

A lighthouse keeper named Tom Bridges described in his autobiography the time he and his family travelled on a night train, a mixed service known as 'The Morepork', all the way from Auckland to Opua. Bridges had been transferred to oversee the lighthouse at Cape Reinga and even if he and his family had been sound asleep, half of Whangarei was probably roused by the sound of the train.[2]

The Opua Express continues due north through Kamo and the old coalmining town of Hikurangi, before curving to the northwest towards Otiria Junction. Like Waiotira Junction, Otiria is full of character — and characters. It is the northernmost junction of the New Zealand network and the final refreshment stop on the journey. The Bay of Islands is just a few more kilometres down the track and appetites surge. Pandemonium reigns in the refreshment rooms and a large, lolloping woman with a voice as piercing as the engine's whistle restores a semblance of order, as customers are herded like bewildered sheep. Passengers are still used to wartime regimentation, and it will take some years for that to ease. In 1946 most remain in high spirits despite the drill-sergeant vocalisations.

Otiria's rail traffic manoeuvrings can be confusing to the uninitiated. The branch to Okaihau, via Kaikohe, heads west from here. Unlike the more conventional arrangements at Waiotira, with a separate local branch line train waiting to carry passengers to Dargaville, at Otiria the Opua Express morphs into two distinct trains. The rear carriages and guard's van are uncoupled from the main body of the train and a second locomotive makes the connection with this configuration, creating the train to Okaihau. Meanwhile the remaining section prepares to take the Opua route.

It had been a puzzling feature of the train, as it departed Auckland, to see two guard's vans attached — one at the tail, the other behind the engine. Some wag suggested that, with so many exuberant holidaymakers and kids on board, the railways needed two guards to keep everyone in check. Two guards, two guard's vans. When the two trains at Otiria were assembled out of one everything made sense.

The terminus of the Okaihau branch being at Okaihau didn't make much sense though. It was an isolated rural settlement of 500 people in the middle of another Northland nowhere, although it could make the claim of being the northernmost station on the New Zealand network. The idea of course, was to extend the line to Kaitaia in the far north but the usual combination of political prevarication and poor funding left the line dangling at Okaihau, or more specifically at Rangiahua, a few kilometres further on. The people of Kaikohe, a much larger town just south of Okaihau, utilised the connection and the Okaihau connection was more about serving them.

With the slimmed-down Opua Express heading for the sea, there was one more rail novelty for the passengers to experience.

Kawakawa, halfway between Otiria and Opua, was a remarkable town, if simply for the fact that the line travelled down the centre of the main thoroughfare, Gillies Street. Shoppers and shopkeepers stopped their daily business to salute the express. Passengers were literally transported by the novelty. Pubs and groceries, tea rooms and garages and a general store or two all seemed close enough to reach out and touch. A handful of workmen, now knocked off and enjoying the rigours of the six o'clock swill, wandered out of the public bar to offer a toast to the Opua Express and all those who travelled on her. On board it really did feel as though the train had jumped the tracks and was running remarkably smoothly down the main road. Either that or it had been mistakenly switched to an old coal mining siding that was here before the shops and other commercial buildings went up.

After all, Kawakawa and its environs is also associated with a unique

A funny way to go shopping? Kids come out to wave as the Opua Express trundles down the main street of Kawakawa.

ATL-WA-36708-F

railway history based on coal extraction and transport. A short spur, from the coal mines of Kawakawa to the wharf at Taumarere, was the first line built anywhere in the North Island. That was in 1868, which seemed an awfully long time ago now as the train skirted the Bay of Islands and passed through the eighteenth and last tunnel.

Peter McCaughan recalls his first encounter, in 1946, with the Kawakawa oddity and the Opua Express.

> Dad deviated off the Opua-Paihia road to show us the township of Kawakawa. We drove down a slight hill and turned left into the main street of the town. Here we were greeted by the sight of a great behemoth hissing and spewing smoke and steam as it proceeded along the centre of the road towards us. My brother and I were quite apprehensive as we had never seen such an object in the middle of the road in all our previous

> travels. We wondered where our father was taking us. It turned out to be nothing more than the Opua Express travelling along the rail line towards Opua. To the locals it was quite normal. With the line situated in the middle of the main street it occurred several times a day.

As the train pulled into the unpretentious Opua station near the wharf at 5.15pm, the sparkling Bay of Islands beckoned. The express was about ten minutes late but up here, time suddenly takes a back seat. One trim matron, who had been concerned that the men drinking at the Kawakawa pub may have downed tools early and taken to the demon drink before 5 o'clock when most workplaces closed, did a silent recalculation. Perhaps the men had been within their rights after all. But really, who cared? The Opua Express had entered a different time zone, where clockwatching was frowned upon. In 1946, with wartime memories receding, it was a doubly enchanting place to be, a paradise, both physically and emotionally.

The Bay of Islands spreads out before the weary traveller, lifting spirits. The winterless north may feel a little less summery than anticipated as a stiff, cool breeze assails alighting passengers, but it cannot detract from the matchless scenery. Thomas Bracken, the New Zealand poet who wrote the lyrics for 'God Defend New Zealand', once described the Bay of Islands as the 'Bay of Beauty'.[3]

For those heading to Russell there are still ferry and road connections to be made. Russell offers idyllic scenery for the sedentary and contemplative, and big game fishing for a new breed of aficionado. Zane Grey and his entourage drew attention to the new sport and now there are many more, both international and New Zealand tourists, who have been drawn to the deep water playground. The part played by the Opua Express in developing the area's reputation as a scenic wonder and fishing paradise has been considerable. It was an 'Angler's El Dorado' according to Grey.

An Englishman, Capt. L. D. Mitchell, who was part of Grey's retinue, at one stage held the world record for catching the largest fish with a rod and line. His prize catch, a black marlin, weighed 443 kg and inevitably a fishy tale or two emerged on the back of his singular effort. It may well have taken Captain Mitchell four hours to finally land the prize catch, but claims that his launch was dragged more than 20 km out to deeper water probably err on the side of exaggeration. Just a tad.

The international reputation of the Bay of Islands was enhanced by the excellence of its fishing grounds and if publications such as the *Auckland Weekly News* could be credited with spreading the word to the wider world, the Opua Express played an equally vital part as a comfortable, steady means of accessing the waters where the big fish were jumping. Northland was well-known, infamous in fact, for its lack of an adequate road network and until improvements were made in later decades, the express continued to attract heavy patronage, even though it only ran three days a week.

Novelist Zane Grey, a 'big fish' from America, enjoys the 'Angler's El Dorado' of New Zealand's big-game fishing.

ATL-1/2-044545-F

From the wharf at Opua, boats, ferries and launches transferred fishermen to newly developed fishing rendezvous. Otehei Bay on Urupukapuka Island was particularly popular. Some big names were now frequenting the area in search of big game. Many were successful. Mr H. White Wickham, of London, secured a hammerhead shark and a broadbill, Lord Grimthorpe of Leeds managed a mako shark and General Sir Thomas Bridges, England, a thresher shark. Not to be outdone, Mr H. A. Britton of Taihape secured a black marlin to keep the local flag flying.

Many famous people travelled on the Opua Express in its heyday, yet the train itself produced a celebrity of its own. A popular guard on the express retired to the Bay of Islands, where he became a well-known New Zealand character. As a tour guide on the famous 'cream trip' launch run between the islands of the Bay of Islands, 'Kewpie' became such a well-known identity tourist boats were named after him.

When the Duke of York visited New Zealand in 1927 he travelled north on the train to the end of the line, to try his hand in the hope of something substantial on the end of his fishing line. The Duke was so enamoured of his experience he made it known that one day he would like to return for a month to do justice to the fishing wonderland, although he never made it.

As well as the Duke, the Bay of Islands catered for a growing number of more ordinary fishermen, women and children, who hankered after smaller fish to fry — boating, swimming, tramping and generally appreciating a wonderful holiday environment. In 1946, especially, it was time to drop a line in the bay and dump a load of cares. The part played by the Opua Express in accessing such a maritime paradise should never be underestimated.

My friend Russell Young, a train-travelling accountant, recalls:

> I have vivid memories of the Opua Express. It was a common means during the period from 1946 to 1956, of undertaking our annual trips to Taipa in the far north, where my parents and us six children would meet up with our many cousins. We travelled initially on the Wellington to Auckland Express from Te Kuiti then changed to the Northland line at Auckland. They were marathon journeys, starting at Te Kuiti Railway Station at 3am and arriving at Taipa around 9pm the same day.
>
> The Express arrived in Auckland around 7.30am and we had time for breakfast before boarding the Opua Express. As a family we did not often venture out into crowded public places and I recall witnessing an altercation between a drunk man and his irate wife. There was much loud bellowing, a large packet of fish and chips was thrown, firstly at the wife, then from wife to drunkard, to everywhere. It was an ugly and shocking spectacle for a four year old to witness.
>
> Luckily the fish and chip throwers didn't catch the Opua Express. It was a settled, if exciting ride. There was a never-ending string of mostly Maori place names. I noted these down in my diary. The train stopped at virtually every station and family groups would board or retire from the train. It was obviously a community lifeline, flowing across wetlands,

> skirting extensive mangrove swamps and giving access to wild, remote areas. At that time there were no tarsealed roads anywhere in Northland and travelling by Bedford bus, which we had to do for the final leg of the journey, led to frequent vomiting. One of my brothers started puking before the bus even arrived. It was a pity the Opua Express, a holiday highlight, didn't run all the way to Taipa.

In 1946, even with the war over, life threw up everyday frustrations. Squirming kids, travel sickness, but most things now seemed to be coated with a veneer of resignation and relief. The words of 'God Defend New Zealand' were no longer a desperate prayer. Besides, we still sang 'God Save the King', although that was slowly changing. The ongoing business of just who would defend New Zealand still continued to rankle a little.

Beyond 1946 New Zealand continued to look to Britain and Europe for several years, but a significant break with tradition occurred when Britain asked New Zealand to contribute to military operations in the Middle East. The latter was considered to be the next centre of conflict, with its vast oil supplies and strategic communications and transport route via the Suez Canal. Russia, a new threat, could be expected to have an eye on such rich resources. New Zealand declined the invitation to send troops to the Middle East, and in following decades concentrated its defence operations in Asia, from whence the Japanese had most recently come. Gradually our defensive allegiance to Britain receded and our troops stayed home, until 1950, when at the behest of the United Nations, New Zealand sent troops to fight in the Korean War.

Meanwhile, the waters of the Bay of Islands lapped languidly at the sea wall, little more than a stone's throw from where the Opua Express rested. Kiwis cavorted in the sun and the fish were biting.

4 Taking the waters and the train

The Rotorua Limited, 1930

The AB engine backed onto the train amidst bedlam. The platform of Auckland Railway Station was awash with passengers preparing to climb on board, and their well-wishers, some perhaps wishing they could join the happy throng preparing for the almost seven-hour journey.

Seven hours was nothing, compared to the overnight express to Wellington. Besides, as a daylight trip it promised rural landscapes and lively vignettes in small towns along the route, not to mention a close look at the burgeoning centre of Hamilton, where the train would turn due east towards Rotorua, its final destination.

Rotorua, the 'Thermal Wonderland of New Zealand' had become a Mecca for tourists and holidaymakers. Overseas visitors made it an almost mandatory stop, and the much-touted means of getting there was the Rotorua Express. Auckland's first express when it was introduced in 1894, and now, in 1930, renamed the Rotorua Limited, the service attracted both attention and keen patronage. Despite hard times in New Zealand, the train, with its gleaming steel carriages of Midland Red provided a diversion for those who dreamed of better days, and a luxurious means of conveyance for the less deprived.

It was a far cry from the days when passenger trains often represented quantity rather than quality. As the train headed beyond Remuera through Ellerslie, memories were cast back to 1885, and a remarkable day. A packed race train from Auckland to Ellerslie carried numerous punters to the racecourse. After the races they joined the return train, that had been long enough in its own right but now, combined with another train, had seven engines tugging at a bewildering array of carriages. Further casual bets were immediately lodged on the likelihood of the snaking return service being the longest train ever assembled on the main Auckland line.

Opposite

A streamlined KA 940 at the head of the Rotorua Express in Hamilton, 1951. The Limited was now known as the Express again.

J.A.T. Terry Photo

The Rotorua Express was a train of firsts. Not only had it been Auckland's first express, but it was the first to feature dining cars with catering services provided by the Railways Department. And now, in 1930, it was the first to flaunt steel carriages with enclosed vestibules between carriages. It was now possible to walk the length of the train without having to negotiate the vagaries of wind and weather. On other trains open-air platforms between carriages did nothing for women's hairdos and a chap had to clasp his fedora firmly, or see it flick off in the downdraft and disappear into someone's back yard or into an impenetrable expanse such as the Whangamarino wetlands — perhaps even a steaming mud pool or bubbling sump as the train approached Rotorua.

On trains composed of the old wooden carriages with open-air balconies, passengers often confined themselves to their own carriage, for fear of being jostled or dampened down by nature and the train's own vortex. On the Rotorua Limited, with its ease of passage, it made perfect sense to merge with passengers from neighbouring carriages, or wander off to take advantage of the observation car located at the end of the train. The observation car was another highlight — the icing on the cake really — and with its lounge chairs arranged spaciously and decorously, provided a further touch of luxury.

From the observation car it was possible, between reading a daily newspaper or a novel, to gaze out the window to the dusty roads, along which the new threat to rail travel, the motorcar, appeared to be struggling to keep up with the smoothly running train. It was easy enough to feel smug and somewhat worldly. Admittedly, New Zealand Railways had made strenuous efforts to improve long-distance passenger services, in the face of increasing car ownership. Despite the fact that the numbers were stacking up — in 1924 over 71,000 motorcars had been registered and by the early 1930s the number had all but doubled — the Rotorua Limited presented a brilliant new face to rail travellers.

In the swank observation car, with its feel of a high-class hotel lounge or lobby, it was difficult to believe the encroachment of coughing, shuddering motorcars on as yet unsealed roads could diminish the influence of rail travel. It certainly couldn't match the grandeur of the Rotorua Limited as it sped on its way.

The main trunk line stretches out ahead. The train heads southwest and

Bookstalls like this one at Frankton provided newspapers, magazines and even novels for the long journey ahead.

HCL-02543 (Daniell Album)

soon the built-up areas recede, revealing green paddocks and small towns. Beyond Drury the Rotorua Limited steams southeastward towards the market garden town of Pukekohe, and further on to Tuakau, located a few kilometres from where the ever-widening Waikato River heads towards its rendezvous with the Tasman Sea. The main trunk avoids having to cross the river at this point by angling back towards Pokeno and the Whangarata Hills.

Many first-time passengers have been anticipating the prospect of accompanying the Waikato River, the country's longest, as the line hugs the river bank for a considerable distance south of Auckland. When the river fails to appear beyond Tuakau there is discernible disappointment. However, as the train slows at Mercer, all is forgiven. Off to the west the river suddenly appears. Admittedly a few kilometres further on, just beyond Meremere, the river disappears as suddenly as it had emerged, but now there are the fascinations of the Whangamarino wetlands to contemplate. For several kilometres the train eases through an area of swamp, limpid pools and dense, often dangling vegetation. Birdlife thrives in this wilderness and the passengers are captivated by the fact that such an unheralded treasure lies on the rail route to Rotorua. Few, if any, roads traverse the backwater and the Whangamarino Swamp, along with the bird's eye view of the Waikato River, has already rendered the trip memorable.

Beyond Te Kauwhata and the massive Lake Waikare, the river returns to accompany the train all the way through Huntly and Ngaruawahia. At Huntly, a junction town, a bridge over the Waikato can be seen jutting out to the west. Some passengers think the main trunk is finally obliged to cross the massive expanse of water, while others, more knowledgeable, realise the river bridge carries the Glen Afton branch, a line serving the coal mines to the west of the town. Coal trains clatter across the bridge, along with miners' trains and those used by general passengers.

Coal wagons, empty and full, festoon the Huntly yards as grunty shunters make up or break down goods trains. The aura of coal is in the air. As if to signal the fact, the AB at the head of the limited belches a pall of rich coal smoke from its funnel.

Coming into Ngaruawahia the main trunk finally has no option. It crosses the river on a steel bridge to the accompaniment of excited exclamations from those occupying window seats. The river is at once dark and menacing, with a slow, sinister flow, like a massive snake waiting to squeeze the life out of the land. On the other hand, it can also be seen as lazy, languid and life-sustaining, a vital thoroughfare for boats and steamers and a rich source of food for those living near its banks. And if the Waikato looks imposing as it flows beneath the bridge, it becomes even more so a short distance downstream where it meets the not inconsequential Waipa, which has drained a huge swathe of the southern Waikato and northern King Country region all the way from its genesis in the ranges to the southwest of Te Kuiti.

Between Ngaruawahia and the large inland town of Hamilton, passengers reflect on the fascinating passage so far. Many prepare to alight at Frankton or Hamilton; others compose themselves for the traditional rush to the refreshment rooms, particularly those whose stomachs are rumbling.

Hamilton in 1930 was a growing town. A cow-town some reckoned, as much because of its servicing function for the many surrounding dairy farms, as for a reputation of being a little less sophisticated than expected of a town of its size and appointment. As the train draws to a halt at the expansive, bustling Frankton Junction Station, passengers amble like Brown's cows, rather than stampeding sheep, to the wide refreshment rooms. The tucker may be basic but it's of a higher standard than many roadside cafeterias. The tea and coffee are streets ahead of what you'd find at the time in New Zealand hotels. And a touch of sophistication is added to culinary arrangements in the form of very popular luncheon hampers. Wicker baskets replete with cold ham, mutton, corned beef or tongue (the latter considered a delicacy), salad, bread, butter, cheese and biscuits filled a void for the hungry traveller. An apple, orange or banana complemented the feast, all washed down with the contents of your own NZR thermos flask of tea. Such luxury set you back three shillings but the Rotorua Limited had more well-to-do travellers opting for hampers than other services. You could sense that by the more dignified amble to 'refreshments' at Frankton — it was nothing like the reported chaos of other services.

The lap of luxury. Passengers take the option of a picnic hamper and a New Zealand Railways thermos.

ATL-APG-2093-1/2-G

Some years earlier, the Frankton rooms had been largely sacked by over a thousand passengers off a race-day special, many of whom were much the worse for alcohol. A boisterous time was had of it. Not all punters were winners, but whether they had reason to celebrate or drown sorrows, they certainly presented as difficult customers for the girls and women serving at the counter.

Frankton is a critical junction of the New Zealand Railways organisation, although some travellers were unaware of this while the train was standing at the station. With water tanks now brimming, the AB pulled out, heading south, until with a perceptible lurch it swung east through Hamilton, leaving the main trunk. Hamilton station, serving the heart of town, was located just this side of the main thoroughfare, Victoria Street, where, even in 1930, the level crossing brought the passage of cars, trucks and pedestrians to a standstill. As the train gathered speed and blasted its whistle, the people of central Hamilton nodded knowingly to one another. That would be the Rotorua Express, or the Rotorua Limited as it was now called. Either way, it had become a familiar visitor since 1902, when it was upgraded to a daily service.

Passengers had barely finished their lunch before the train suddenly roared out on to the Claudelands Bridge spanning the Waikato River. It was not unknown for scallywags, school boys and other impolite types to cast their railway cups from the train into the deep waters. Crockery didn't float and no doubt a muddy bounty lined the bottom of the river. Not that anyone on the Rotorua Limited would stoop to such a thing. Besides, the views along the river banks, with grand houses cresting sections sloping down to boat jetties and bungalows looking for all the world like houseboats, such was their proximity to the river, discouraged such ill-mannered tomfoolery.

Beyond the bridge, and the waving home gardeners fossicking in the backyards of Hamilton suburbs, the line followed a straight course beyond the town limits into the dairy flatlands of the eastern Waikato Plains.

At Ruakura Junction on the outskirts of Hamilton, the Cambridge branch headed south. Several passengers expressed surprise. After all,

pivotal role in sparking the tourist boom in Rotorua. Amidst the bustle on Rotorua Station, any doubters would have had their views seriously challenged. The Rotorua Limited, the 'New Train De Luxe' of the rail promotion brochures and posters, is still enabling out-of-towners, local and overseas tourists, country folk and Aucklanders to live the dream driven by the Government Tourist Department and New Zealand Railways, in symbiotic combination.

Rotorua Station is resplendent with striking promotional posters propounding the advantages of train travel. 'New Zealand — Paradise of the Pacific' is a particularly eye-catching declaration, but many other such inducements have played a part in spinning the Rotorua tourist wheel.

The part played by the New Zealand Railway Studios, established in 1920, is here for the world to see. Indeed, much of the promotional material and stamps, not to mention the matchless posters that turned the medium into a virtual art form, found their way overseas. This probably accounts for the sprinkling of foreign accents heard at Rotorua Station. Americans drawled, Australians twanged. Stately English couples enquired, in clipped tones, about luggage arrangements and hotel bookings. The strong accents of Europeans — Polish, French — caused a few communication problems, but a knot of Maori women, resplendent with moko and pipes, were happy to sit and watch and pass comment in their own tongue.

Of thermal wonders and 'lovely lakes'. A poster extolling the virtues of rail excursions to Rotorua.

ATL-Eph-D-TOURISM-1927-01

It was a scene of joyous chaos in some quarters, quiet anticipation in others. It was perhaps noticeable that the more formally attired were 'seen to' before other passengers, although virtually without exception, alighting visitors were nowhere near scruffy in appearance. As if to provide contrast, and to remind all of the parlous times visiting the less fortunate, a gaggle of swaggers, shiftless men who wandered the country looking for work and warmth, stood watching the unloading of the train.

As the melee gradually eased, some passengers were already booking return seats in the booking hall, queuing with those travellers who had been in town for however long their circumstances allowed, and were now reluctantly arranging their journeys home. They looked relaxed and contented. Rotorua had worked its charms. Some women in fur coats and wrappers snuggled affectionately into husbands — or were they boyfriends or bounders encountered in the magical city? The somewhat vague notion of the romantic railways assumed a rather direct implication, even as an advertisement for James Cowan's well-written guide, 'Romance of the Rail' adorned the wall. Elsewhere posters encouraged further patronage as did enticing, colourful maps of the New Zealand rail network. Interesting deals such as 'Half-fares for Whole People' were on offer. Sunday trains were available too, prompting one wag, an Australian by the sound of him, to ponder the notion of 'Half-fares for holy people'.

If the train journey and the experience of Rotorua Station had been bewitching enough, what lay in store in Rotorua and its hinterland would soon live up to all the palaver and expectation. Taking the waters, and enjoying the calming pleasures of Rotorua's spas and bath-houses, drew thousands. The bubbling thermal waters were able to draw out whatever ailed the unwell and invigorate the hale and hearty. Tourists from the mother country, in particular, took a fancy to the spas of Empire. Rotorua was a jewel in the crown, even more so than accessible European hot spots. Dr A. S. Wohlman, appointed in 1902 as the Government Balneologist, had concentrated his efforts on the curative and relaxing thermal spas of Rotorua. When he retired in 1919 he laid claim to the astounding figure of 2.5 million baths having been administered in Rotorua by his staff. By 1930, despite hard times, thousands still immersed themselves, including those carried to the town by train.

Of course there was more to it than that. Rotorua also provided spectacular scenic options. Some of the thermal water and mud pools were dangerously hot and, thankfully, few availed themselves of an unsolicited dip. Also only for looking at were geysers, which spouted metres into the sulphurous air. If any reminder were needed of the potential fury of the district, a trip to the Buried Village, created by the destruction in 1886 of a former attraction, the Pink and White Terraces, was both fascinating and sobering. Then there were the lakes — not just Rotorua, but Rotoiti, Rotoma and Tarawera — where bathing, fishing, boating and sightseeing were popular. The hotels and guesthouses were lively and usually full, as were some of the more foolhardy guests. But most sipped contemplatively on their gin and tonics and sherries, soaking up the town and its charms, and reflecting on the unexpected scenic delights.

Auckland-born author H. Hector Bolitho wrote:

> We expected sulphur smells and steaming holes and were not disappointed. But we did not expect to find the door to Hades surrounded by beautiful lakes and tree covered hills. All sense of terror or ugliness is removed by the nearness of the rivers, lakes and valleys. In the cool of the evening, which could more aptly be termed the 'cold', we stepped onto Rotorua Station where silk hats and frock coats told us that it was to be a smart little town with a dignity all its own.[1]

When in Rotorua, one of the standard dalliances was to amble down to the station to enjoy the quiet pandemonium of departing and arriving trains, whether you were travelling or not. When the time did come to leave, many opted for the return Rotorua Limited, with its connections at Morrinsville for those wishing to travel to Thames and Tauranga and Frankton, from which point main trunk services reached Wellington via Waitomo, of glow-worm caves fame, and National Park and its mountains.

Others, aware that Rotorua was the railhead, opted for bus services to continue their journey through New Zealand. They would have preferred to continue by train to Taupo or the Pacific Coast but if there were serious plans for lines south and west of Rotorua, they were soon shelved as the encroachment of motorcars and buses gathered pace.

While 1930 may have seen the upgrading of the Rotorua Express to Limited, it also witnessed the daunting business of the installation of a Manager of Combined Road Motor Services in both the North and South Islands. It may have been ironic that New Zealand Railways was making such appointments, but it was also a prescient indication that the petrol-driven revolution was gaining momentum.

Meanwhile the Rotorua Limited continued to bathe in its justifiable glory. And bathing in the hot pools, and the taking of the waters, afforded a certain hilarity amongst returning passengers as the train prepared to pull out of Rotorua. While most travellers settled in for a sedate and seemly gambol along the lake frontage before the AB climbed away from paradise, more rakish elements recalled reports of naked males dunking themselves in the pools. This was out of order, according to regulations, and the perpetrators were asked to leave. Next day they returned to the baths with their bathing trunks tied around their necks. This complied technically with the rules, for the latter did not specify which part of the anatomy had to accommodate the trunks. On hearing of such larks, upper lips stiffened. Not a few ladies within earshot blushed. 'It wouldn't do for the Duke, sir,' a traveller suggested in an upper-crust British accent.

He could of course have been referring to the fact that the first fully fledged royal train, carrying the Duke and Duchess of Cornwall and York in 1901, followed the course of the Rotorua Express. The Duke and Duchess were later installed as King George V and Queen Mary. The Rotorua Express became the Rotorua Limited, itself a prince among New Zealand passenger trains. And similar reprobates, like the ones who chortled at the naked pool romps, no doubt later busted their sides about 'seeing Queen Mary's bottom'. In truth the cruise liner *Queen Mary* did have a bottom, but in 1930 it was still being built.

At 10.10am, the departure time from Rotorua — a most civilised time to take a train after a bit of a lie-in and leisurely breakfast — a moving geyser erupted. That was the AB engine, letting off steam as it drew the return train away from the tree-fringed station and set about making it

'God Save the King'. An engine all dolled up for the coronation of King Edward VII in 1902.

HCL-04302

back to Auckland by 4pm, before dark at any time of year. The limited number of stops — seven, as opposed to 17 on the express — facilitated its flight and gave it its new 'limited' name. As the train turned its back on Ngongotaha and set about climbing to Mamaku, at an altitude of 574 m, the lake sparkled with a new sheen as steam from the countless hot springs around the shore rose 'in snowy clouds like the smoke of enchanted camp fires'. At least that's how writer James Cowan described the scene. Another traveller on the train summed up the Rotorua hinterland, our 'Geyserland in Paradise', as being more absorbing than America's Yellowstone Park. It was more compact and accessible.[2]

And now, with the introduction of the new Rotorua Limited, there was a means of travel that did justice to its illustrious destination point. It was just a matter of deciding which was more pleasurable: the train journey itself, or the romps and attractions after arrival.

Once the Siver Fern, then the Geyserland, and after that … nothing. The Geyserland passes the Kaimai Express.

D.R. Simpson

Thanks to the resurgence of passenger rail services in the 1990s I was finally able to travel on the fabled route of the Rotorua Limited, when Tranzscenic instituted several new services more specifically aimed at the tourist market. Given Rotorua's continuing status as a vital cog in our tourist machinery, a train from Auckland to Rotorua via Hamilton seemed to have every chance of success.

Like the Kaimai Express, another 1990s invention, the Geyserland service utilised former Silver Fern railcars. The new service was no faithful reproduction of the name train that excited the imagination all those years ago, but it was sleek and well-maintained and kept to schedules.

In keeping with its contemporary status, a flying wedge of Asian tourists alighted from the train at Hamilton and, honouring the past, a voluble group of English travellers took their place. The Geyserland was well patronised and efficiently run, but a certain sameness had prevailed for us until the train pulled out of Hamilton Station. Until now we had been travelling down the main trunk, a line as familiar to us as old boots. However, beyond the curved island platform on the Bay of Plenty line the journey took on a new dimension. We were heading directly for the Waikato River, but not before the line descended into darkness on the fringes of the city's CBD.

In the days of the Rotorua Limited the line travelled through the heart of the city, with the arrival of the train causing much coming and going and to-ing and fro-ing. As the numbers of motorcars and trucks increased over the years the disruption to everyday traffic at the level crossing on Victoria Street became a hindrance. While small boys delighted in watching the train steam past, they didn't have to bear the commercial and logistical consequences. Inevitably, with the continued growth of the city, thoughts were expressed about limiting or circumnavigating the problem. Eventually, in 1964, a new underground line and station opened and the only downtown evidence of passing trains was an ominous rumbling in shops and malls as eastbound trains burrowed beneath the streets.

Hamilton railway tunnel, just beyond the Waikato River, 2010. Part of a ghost railway in terms of regular passenger services.

Graham Hutchins

The new underground Hamilton Station served a useful purpose for a number of years when railcars still travelled on the Bay of Plenty line, but in 1994 the decision was made to close the station, because of vandalism and threats to passenger safety.

There was already a feeling of constriction and cutting back along the old route of the Rotorua Limited, when in 1989 the lines were lifted beyond suburban Koutu Station in Rotorua. It was no longer possible to terminate your journey at the old central Rotorua site. Despite the fact that Rotorua still abounded in thermal wonders and tourist attractions, the part played by the railways in serving them had receded.

In October, 2001 the Geyserland railcar ceased operations and the line to Rotorua has been bereft of regular passenger services ever since.

5 Train to nowhere

The Taneatua Express, 1939

Taneatua is a small eastern Bay of Plenty town located 50 km southwest of Opotiki and just under 15 km south of Whakatane. More significantly, it is all of 384 km from the city of Auckland. In 1952 it boasted a population of 437 and owed its existence to the cutting up, in 1896, of the Opouriao Estate. In 1939 it numbered about a hundred fewer people.

Sited at the junction of the Whakatane and Waimana Rivers, it is a service town for local dairy farming and more generalised land use. More than anything though, in 1939 it was the railhead for a unique and much-loved passenger train. The Taneatua Express, running all the way from the big smoke, concluded its journey in the humble town. Because it was so close to the Pacific Ocean visitors were perplexed to find Taneatua nestling in a lonely inland valley. Such a 'name' train should, you would have thought, conclude its long scenic journey at a location overlooking the crashing surf or in a charming seaside town famous for coves and bays.

Whakatane or Opotiki seemed the obvious railheads, but the North Island East Coast line had loftier intentions. On the other side of the broken country beyond Taneatua, the Moutuhora branch reaching beyond the city of Gisborne came to an abrupt halt in the middle of nowhere. The intention had been to link the Moutuhora line with Taneatua but political and financial constraints over the years had left both ends of the line dangling. Auckland to Gisborne was the plan, but as a result not a few first-time travellers found themselves in Taneatua, a less than overwhelming destination.

Not that Taneatua wasn't a friendly place, with an equal proportion of Maori and Europeans, a licensed hotel and several boarding houses. At least travellers would not be obliged to build a bivouac in the bush for an overnight stay. Besides, if there were passengers who hankered after a spot of river fishing and hunting, Taneatua was as good a place as any to indulge such passions. Motor services connected with Gisborne through the Waioeka Gorge, and anyway, the bush and river scenery was appealing in itself. It's just that Taneatua wasn't the sort of terminus travellers expected at the end of a long often spectacular journey through South Auckland, the Waikato and a good slice of the Bay of Plenty.

Opposite

The AB-hauled Taneatua Express crossing the Claudelands bridge in Hamilton in 1948.

J.A.T. Terry Photo

Most popular New Zealand express trains ran from city to city. And when they didn't, like the Auckland to Opua train, at least the line ended at the edge of the ocean, where travellers were beguiled by the tourist delights of the Bay of Islands. The Central Otago Express from Dunedin might have concluded at the small inland town of Cromwell, but the scenic playgrounds of Queenstown and Lake Wanaka lay tantalisingly close, down connecting roads.

The Taneatua Express was all about the towns and cities it served on its long meander. The final stretch to Taneatua was essentially a matter of rail authorities utilising the line because it went that far. That's not to suggest that the townsfolk of Taneatua didn't avail themselves of the rail service, but there was little in the way of departure bedlam at the modest station. A population of 600-plus could generate only so much patronage. And still there were first-time travellers, foreign tourists in particular, who set out from the other end of the line at Auckland with the justifiable intention of descending on Taneatua as if it harboured a harbour or the sort of magic for which Rotorua was famous. After all, the name sounded exotic.

One sunny summer's day in 1939, an AB locomotive backed on to a line of carriages waiting at Auckland Station. The passengers boarding the Taneatua Express were a more homely, less formally attired bunch than those who had caught the Rotorua Limited, already departed; in fact, even the Opua Express clientele presented a more opulent aspect. The Taneatua Express accommodated mainly family groups. Excited kids and parents, mustering their flocks like sheepdogs, took their places. Some passengers, heading only as far as Hamilton, preferred the Taneatua Express to the Rotorua train because it left at the less ungodly hour of 9.08am.

That's not to say that there weren't well-dressed, decorous couples heading for Tauranga, the 'Riviera of the South', edging uneasily around the scrums of boisterous children clogging the aisles.

It was a good-sized train, far too big if it was serving Taneatua alone, but it pulled out efficiently, even though it left a minute or two late because some kid had left his bucket and spade outside the ladies' waiting room. There was also general dithering by a gaggle of senior citizens.

For many travellers the stretch of main trunk between Auckland and Hamilton was well known. Holidaymakers spent a good deal of the three hours until refreshments at Frankton chattering and yelling animatedly. And that was only the parents. Some children, boys mainly, skidded up and down the aisle until one young bounder went headfirst into the side of an old lady's seat. He ended up with a bloodied nose and a firm admonishment from the guard.

The guard had his work cut out in other carriages too, but by the time the train passed Pokeno, just beyond Tuakau, a relative calm had descended. It was now possible to contemplate the fate of a long-proposed and promised connecting line from Pokeno to Paeroa, which would significantly reduce travelling times between Auckland and the east coast. As early as 1914 expectations had been raised regarding a link across the Hauraki Plains,

The serious business of getting to the beach is reflected in the face of the boy at the carriage window. The Taneatua Express near Morrinsville, 1949.

J.A.T. Terry Photo

shortening the Auckland – Paeroa trip by as much as 64 km. Construction was authorised in 1919, only to have work delayed by heavy flooding on the swampy recesses of the Hauraki Plains.

If doubters figured the authorities had no real intention of proceeding with the line they would have been rendered less cynical when extensive realignment of the Paeroa rail yards went ahead, necessary if trains were to travel directly through to Pokeno. Of course the Depression years caused delays, but in 1938 the first sod was turned in a ceremony that reconfirmed the seriousness of the railways' commitment. Then another war broke out — World War II — and although 24 km of construction, most of it between Pokeno and Maramarua, had been completed, wartime manpower shortages led to suspension of the operation.

Further down the main trunk, Mercer, Huntly and Ngaruawahia saw the Taneatua Express make good time. On 13 August 1877, the line between Mercer and Ngaruawahia was opened to considerable fanfare. A 30-carriage train hauled by three locos carried 200 passengers, including officials, along the mint track. There was a slight delay when the leading engine hit a pair of horses that had wandered onto the line near the Maungawara Bridge. The iron horse prevailed and sadly the flesh and blood horses were killed.

Spirits were raised again as Mr Simon Fraser, who had been playing his bagpipes, continued his hornpipes, jigs, strathspeys and reels. Spirits were raised in other ways as bottles of whisky were opened to toast the splendid new passage south. Was the whisky to blame when the line and train appeared to carry on south of Ngaruawahia, or had the engine brakes failed? Were the drivers succumbing to one toast too many? The line only went as far south as Ngaruawahia, so was the monstrous train now ghosting over flat, line-less land? It was later revealed that for some reason the station had been constructed almost a kilometre closer to Hamilton than was practical. Eventually another station was built in the centre of Ngaruawahia, but a strange duplicity prevailed for some years after the line reached Hamilton. Northbound trains stopped at the outlying satellite station, while those heading south used the central structure. By 1897 the latter was known as

Ngaruawahia Station, while the other became the goods station. Perhaps station plans had been drawn up during whisky-washed consultations.[1]

In 1939 passengers were feeling parched by the time the Taneatua Express reached Frankton Junction. And hungry. The refreshment rooms fairly rocked with the footfall of refreshments seekers. It was a little after midday. The Taneatua Express, since its inception in 1928, had become a popular means for families to travel to the seaside at Tauranga, Mount Maunganui and other beaches. At a time when cars and buses were fewer, and roads remained dusty, winding and vomit-inducing for some sensitive young stomachs, the express carried landlocked central North Islanders to popular, white-sand East Coast beaches. Many such passengers joined the train at Frankton. Some years later Russell Young recalled a trip he and his family made.

> At Christmas, 1954, we broke from our far north holiday tradition, and were provided with a bach at Mount Maunganui instead. By this time the two eldest children in the family had left home so it was a smaller group that departed Te Kuiti Railway station at a more leisurely hour of 5.30am on the overnight limited and alighted at Frankton Junction. Here we walked through to the adjacent platform to board the Taneatua Express. I recall the excitement of crossing the Claudelands Bridge over the Waikato River and seeing a number of small craft. There were frequent stops. At Paeroa a second engine was attached to the rear of the train, so at times you could look along the train and see an engine at each end. There is a memorable tunnel exit in the middle of the Karangahake Gorge, where the train arrows out from a rock face and on to a bridge with huge girders, the river in foaming flood below. The line shared the bridge with the road. Another exciting part was the Athenree Gorge with its frequent bridges spanning the snaking road below. I remember extensive mangrove swamps along the Apata – Te Puna section. There was a lengthy stop at Tauranga before we crossed the harbour bridge. The train ran down to Mount Maunganui to enable us to alight before it headed on down the coast to

> Taneatua. I always found the name 'Taneatua Express' pretty exciting — it sounded like a really important place. It wasn't until many years later that I found out there is almost nothing at all at Taneatua.

The mysteries of Taneatua prevailed as the train pulled out of Frankton after a good twenty minute break. Some passengers had enjoyed a sit-down meal in the dining room, although this facility was to close in 1954, the year Russell Young and his family travelled on the express. At Claudelands the train said goodbye to the Waikato River, and at Ruakura the line to Cambridge headed south.

Many years before the Cambridge branch had been approved by government, but not without overcoming opposition. Sir George Grey and his party were not in favour, although earlier the Minister of Public Works and members of the House of Representatives had expressed guarded enthusiasm. Further approaches eventually resulted in the Cambridge Railway Bill being passed. Construction of the line took less than a year and was one of the most straight, and straightforward, branches rail engineers faced in this country.

The real essence of the Taneatua Express set in after Morrinsville, as the Bay of Plenty line headed towards the Kaimai Ranges. After the familiarity of the main trunk from Auckland to Frankton, and the flatness and occasional monotony of the eastward trek across the wide Waikato Plains, the cut through the Karangahake Gorge was a timely reminder of just how skilled and intrepid the engineers and construction workers had been when they hacked out a course through the ranges.

Prior to that the pleasures of Te Aroha, with its hot springs nestled beneath the towering Mount Te Aroha, and Paeroa Junction, with its interesting rail perambulations, held the attention. At around 2pm Paeroa Junction was 'time for refreshments'. The line to Thames continued northwards while the passage of the Taneatua Express headed east, after the engine was realigned. The tracks from the Waikato and the east met at the junction in the form of an inverted V shape. The train was now set to travel 'backwards' with the guard's van next to the engine. This oddity had long been castigated by those who considered it to be a time-waster, but those on board, particularly the kids, delighted in the flurry of attendant activity as seat backs were flipped so passengers were not obliged to travel with their backs to the emerging scenic delights. Some family groups already sitting in face to face configurations were not affected, although one young lad who had lost the privilege of seeing what lay ahead first, complained bitterly. Besides travelling backwards made him feel sick, he claimed, although his mother was more inclined to believe the ham sandwich from the refreshment rooms had upset his stomach. Youngsters were often caught unawares by the unpleasant bite of railways' mustard.

An old man, nonplussed by the temporary pandemonium, was heard to curse the cancellation of the Pokeno – Paeroa line. The train would have been in Tauranga by now, he reckoned. Furthermore, Paeroa could have rejoiced in a unique rail status: a junction node that served three, not two lines, with the main line heading east, the Thames branch providing a juxtaposition to the north and the Pokeno Deviation coming in from the west.

The same old man pined for a night service, like the Frankton – Thames railcar that was inaugurated in 1926 — if there were troublesome brats on board they'd be sound asleep and out of harm's way. And sleeping was the quickest means of getting from A to B. The old man had been on the Taneatua Express once too often it seemed. Familiarity had bred contempt.

The Frankton – Thames night passenger service was lauded as one of the most popular trains ever introduced by the Department. A Sentinel-Cammell railcar was utilised on the run that left Frankton Junction at 10.35pm and returned from Thames at 3.15am. It was remarkable for the fact that it was one of the very few instances of a steam railcar being used as a night service over what was virtually a main line. It was certainly the only New Zealand example at the time. It was further praised for its low running costs. Very few station staff would be required (the passengers would be sleeping in their seats), and one shilling a mile, inclusive of driver, fireman and guard's wages, was considered good value compared to conventional

Karangahake Station and the gorge beyond – a region of former gold-mining glories.

J.A.T. Terry Photo

trains. The occasional stray cattle on the line outside and the sporadic troublesome whisky tippler inside, were two of the few impediments to a service that could now expedite delivery of newspapers, most notably the *Auckland Star*. Apparently the service was introduced at the behest of the Auckland newspaper, but the authorities in general took little convincing.

After Paeroa the Karangahake Gorge closes in like a tourniquet. The Ohinemuri River gurgles through, while the road and railway cling to whatever land and ledges remain. This is old gold territory and evidence of former glories is everywhere: decaying stamper batteries, tiny miners' cottages, disused mine sidings and ramshackle towns that once teemed with activity. MacKaytown, Karangahake itself, Owharoa and Waikino pass before the train reaches Waihi.

The Karangahake Gorge possesses a rugged beauty. The Ohinemuri River originates not far from the Bay of Plenty coast and flows through a narrow cleft in the ranges that extend from as far north as Cape Colville to the southern tip of the Kaimais. The narrow, steep-sided gorge is unique in providing the only route through the long line of ranges.

In 1939, as the Taneatua Express eases through, the Victoria gold battery at Waikino is still operating, but is one of the few remnants of a region once world-famous for its methods of gold recovery. The battery at

Karangahake township boasted the world's first field test of the cyanide process in gold extraction. There was serious gold to be had.

Between 1875, when gold was discovered, and 1918, the gorge and its settlements burgeoned. During these years four million pounds worth of gold was claimed. The lure of gold was the principal motivation for advancing the railway between Paeroa, initially as far as Waihi in 1905, with a branch off the then Auckland – Thames line.

Waihi is also the site of the infamous 1912 miners' strike. It was a pivotal moment in the development of the New Zealand Labour movement, out of which the New Zealand Labour Party eventually emerged. Violence erupted between strikers, strike-breakers and policemen. Initially a group of miners were arrested and charged with 'jostling' an engine driver. The magistrate declared they had come 'within an ace of committing an assault'. Events escalated and eventually Frederick George Evans, a miner, was bludgeoned and beaten to death, becoming a martyr to the labour cause. The Federation of Labour's publication, *The Tragic Story of the Waihi Strike*, described Evans as 'a victim to the thuggery of capitalism, a victim to the lawlessness of the law'.[2]

Frederick George Evans, 'a martyr to the labour cause'.

ATL-PAColl-3736

Waihi is also where Nora Dean, a frequent traveller, boarded the train. When Nora caught the Taneatua Express at Waihi between the Karangahake and Athenree Gorges, she was of an age when the history of New Zealand politics and the politics of railway construction were furthest from her mind. The business of not being able to travel all the way through the hills to Gisborne, and even to Hawke's Bay, where she and her family had endured and survived the 1931 Napier earthquake, were now small cheese. Nora's new focus was Whakatane, where she was to take up digs with a kindly woman who lived at Ohope Beach, just beyond the town.

Waihi had been my home town, after we were forced to leave Havelock North because of the Napier earthquake. Now I was off to live in Whakatane. I travelled second class in a smoker's carriage. There were a

> lot of Maori people on board and several were playing their guitars and everyone was singing. During World War II, once darkness fell further along the line, the train windows were blacked out and the guard used a light with a handle when he came through the carriages calling out the names of each stop. The guard looked after us very well.

The train eased beyond Waimata through the Athenree Gorge and soon the vast waters of Tauranga Harbour flickered in the distance. Matakana Island dominated the horizon. Tahawai, Katikati, Aongatete, Apata, Pahoia, Omokoroa (where the line crossed a harbour inlet, eliciting excited noises from children), Borrell, Te Puna and Otumoetai all seemed to flit past before reaching Tauranga, at just after 5pm, and a little late. Time for more refreshments for those staying with the train. Those alighting seem drawn to the glowering cone of Mount Maunganui, described by writer Joyce West as resembling a sandcastle moulded in a child's beach bucket. It is an appropriate likeness; many of the disembarking families will be visiting the ocean beach beyond the dome after they have done with Tauranga.[3]

The final link with Tauranga, in a construction sense, was a long time coming. Excavation had commenced back in 1910 with the short section between Tahawai and the Wairoa River contracted out to Sir W. Armstrong-Whitworth and Co, but the remainder was the preserve of the Public Works Department. Tauranga and East Coast residents looked forward to the line's completion, as inadequate harbour facilities hampered local development. In 1928 the official opening ceremony was subsequently a day for celebration, with 5000 locals taking advantage of the Department's free train service.

The arrival of the first train, carrying the Right Honourable J. G. Coates, Prime Minister and Minister of Railways, who made the journey from Wellington, was greeted with thunderous applause and cheering, and a haka performed by local Maori assembled on the platform.

'You have a great district and great people settled in it,' Prime Minister Coates trumpeted. 'And I hope you will stick to your own railway service.'

The Minister of Public Works intimated that the new railway would lead to a huge improvement and development in the Bay of Plenty. He appealed in particular to Maori to use the line, especially in the transportation of their maize and kumara.

The *New Zealand Railways Magazine* described the final ceremonials of the opening:

> At the conclusion of the speeches Mrs MacMillan cut a ribbon held at the ends by two little girls, pakeha and Maori — Miss Eileen Dive, daughter of the Mayor, and Miss Rangihoie. Cheers were given for Mr B. C. Robbins, secretary of the celebrations committee, whose efforts had so completely been crowned with success.[4]

Prime Minister and Minister of Railways Gordon Coates strikes a jaunty pose, while passing the time with an engine driver.

ATL-PAColl-5469-054

It was Viscount Bledisloe who described Tauranga as the Riviera of the South. It even had a foreign look to it.

In 1937, Joyce West wrote in the *New Zealand Railways Magazine:*

> The architecture of Tauranga is a curious mingling of new and old. The influence of the Spanish Mission is strong, and plaster fronts and sun-tinted pillars jostle half-timbered Tudors and pseudo-English cottages, and all lie cheek by jowl with small starting houses of no particular design, whose windows probably watched the red-coat soldiers march through Tauranga.[5]

From the Strand on the waterfront the rail bridge across the harbour juts out and the many boats and jetties give a Mediterranean feel. After the inland wanderings of the Taneatua Express across the plains and the hemmed-in, if fascinating, ride through the gorges, the ocean aspect and charms of Tauranga are a revelation.

The sun continues to beat down. Even in winter, during May, June and July, this region enjoys more sunshine than most others in the Dominion. Its population is described as being made up of holidaymakers, retired colonels and dairy farmers. Such a combination may have been an odd description, although it helps create the picture of a town with a distinctive character. As the summer months end, 'so ebbs from the town the unrestful tide of young women in slacks and young men in shorts and sandshoes,' wrote Joyce West.[6]

Tauranga was a popular place. The railways had cashed in too, and as well as the Taneatua Express and mixed services, special excursions transported hundreds of out-of-towners. On Saturday, 17 July 1928, a train ran from Paeroa for the benefit of 530 passengers, who filled 13 carriages. Two engines were required. The number of travellers was only three less than the contingent who travelled to Tauranga from Thames the previous Saturday. Four football (rugby) teams, five basketball (netball) teams, a ladies' hockey team and a mixed golf team joined the general public on the Paeroa – Tauranga excursion. All roads — and rails — lead to Tauranga, even in winter.

Nora Dean enjoyed a cup of tea and ham and mustard sandwiches as the engine driver and firemen fussed around their hot charge, perspiration dripping. The AB engine was living up to its reputation as perhaps the most popular steam loco on the New Zealand system.

The Taneatua Express bucked slightly as it left the Strand station and arced out over the Tauranga Harbour rail bridge. The steel truss structure traced a wide semicircle as it linked downtown Tauranga with Matapihi on the other side. The bridge held the distinction of being the longest in the then Auckland Province (a large area extending from Auckland south to New Plymouth and across to northern Hawke's Bay), and was made up of 14 separate spans of 31.7 metres each, adding up to a total length of 443.8 metres.

Kids became restive, particularly those from Auckland, who had endured an eight-hour journey, before realising they were only ten minutes away from release at Te Maunga on the peninsula, where road transport would take them on to seaside baches and guest houses. The temptation to plunge into the froth and foam would be too much for them to endure, certainly beyond any parental exhortations to help unpack.

The engine found a new gear as it headed away. Kids frolicked in the surf as the train left vestiges of its existence: a discernible echo of wheels, a dispersing tower of coal smoke that met the inland clouds, and a long wolf-like howl on the whistle.

Janet Frame, the New Zealand writer, spoke of her experiences at Mount Maunganui and how the meeting with the sea inspired prose as immaculate breakers broke under clear Bay of Plenty moonlight.

The train settled in for a rollicking seaside romp down the coast. Long before the line between Tauranga and Taneatua was opened in 1928, the vast stretch of white sand beaches provided the best means of getting from Tauranga all the way south to Opotiki. In fact it was the only 'road' for many years and took horsemen two days.

In 1939 the railway dallied about inland as it passed through Kairua, Papamoa, Te Puke, Rangiuru, Paengaroa, Maniatutu, Pongakawa, Pukehina and Ohinepanea. Pleasant, fertile dairying paddocks, maize fields and orchards centring on Te Puke, flashed past. The train stopped frequently, but the interruptions were accepted as a vital function of the Taneatua Express, as it set down passengers and papers. At Pongakawa the line crossed the sluggish river that provided passage for Hongi Hika's war canoe as it headed for Arawa territory and the subsequent invasion of a hundred-odd years ago.

Suddenly the line emerges at the ocean near Otamarakau. The lowering sun casts long shadows from the headlands on to the Pacific's blue expanse. From here to Matata the express hugs the coast in a dramatic, prolonged maritime train ride. Comparisons are made with the South Island's northern line along the Kaikoura coast, between Wharanui and Clarence, where construction was continuing south towards Kaikoura township.

At Otamarakau, a great walled pa guards the headland, taking the fancy of historian James Cowan.

> If I were looking for a lovely site for a seaside home and had my pick of coastwise lookouts, I think I should choose this immemorial Maori fortress. A dark little river glides below and empties itself in the vast blue

> bay, underneath a buttress-like salient, cliff and tree-crowned, that must have been the citadel of the entrenched town.[7]

Beyond Pikowai the waves crashed relentlessly as the light began to dim. Matata and its exotic lagoon present another stop. The station is located almost a kilometre out of this old Pakeha-Maori settlement with its native village, clear views of volcanic White Island's steam plumes, and blooming pohutukawa trees. The engine works up its own head of steam as it pulls the train around the headland of the Manawahe hills and across the Rangitaiki Plains. Awakaponga, Otakiri, Edgecumbe, Awakeri — the train keeps stopping as the end of the journey approaches.

This side of Otakiri, a new branch to Kawerau would head further inland when it was opened in 1953, under the auspices of the Ministry of Works. In many ways 1953 was a stellar year for New Zealand. Sir Edmund Hillary climbed Mount Everest, Queen Elizabeth II ascended to the throne and later toured New Zealand with her husband, Prince Phillip, although the All Blacks lost to Wales at the end of the year and the dreadful Tangiwai rail disaster rocked the nation a few days later.

The engine appreciates a drink while the driver appreciates the view. An empty Whakatane Board Mills train at Awakeri, 1951.

J.A.T. Terry Photo

Little Awakeri is a junction now. In 1939 the Whakatane Board Mills opened their own connection with the main line from Whakatane to Awakeri, to expedite the movement of logs and timber. It seemed a thousand pities, Nora Dean mused, that some sort of public passenger connecting service couldn't be trundled down the new branch into Whakatane. Even better, why not re-route the Taneatua Express down the board mill tracks and end its journey at Whakatane? It was a much more significant settlement than Taneatua and, now that the line construction beyond the Taneatua terminus wasn't going ahead, there seemed little point in terminating the train there. As it was, Nora was obliged to leave the train at a station called Whakatane West, which, despite its name, was several kilometres from Whakatane. The train was running half an hour late and at 8pm night was falling.

> When I got off at Whakatane West I had no idea where to go. Just by chance a mail bus was waiting for the train. The driver, a Mr Hooper, wanted to know where I was going and kindly took me to the address in Whakatane I had been given. He mentioned that he didn't usually meet the train on the day I was travelling, so it was a lucky break. Return journeys from Whakatane to Whakatane West were easier though, with a New Zealand Road Service bus connecting with the express.

The Taneatua Express chugged off inland with its remaining handful of patrons. Darkness descended as it reached Tuhoe country. Just this side of Taneatua the line crossed the Whakatane River, although in the dark, the swishing sound of the train on the bridge would have meant little to first-time travellers. Locals prepared to alight, aware of their surroundings. Around 8.30 the train finally pulled into the mysterious Taneatua, where lights twinkled in a cluster of houses and street lamps went on. It had been a long ride, nearly 16 kilometres further than the southern route between Christchurch and Dunedin. The final link from Tauranga had taken over three hours but the handful of passengers didn't seem to mind. Some sought out the bus connections with Opotiki and Gisborne, while a couple of long-haul travellers were directed to a local boarding house. The rest, residents of Taneatua, walked home through the quiet streets. The only sound was that of the exhausted AB engine as it severed its ties with the express and chuffed off to the engine shed.

The sound reminded locals that their small town was often regarded as one of the most important settlements in the North Island, simply because of the Taneatua Express. Several were making preparations to travel on the next train out of town, leaving at 7.45 in the morning. It was funny how their train was referred to as the Taneatua Express, as it headed north beyond Whakatane, yet some passengers insisted on calling it the Tauranga Express as it threaded the gorges before opening out on to the Waikato Plains all the way to Hamilton and Frankton. Heading north on the main trunk it was, to some, now the Hamilton Express. Yet to most it would always be the Taneatua Express.

In 1959, however, the express gave way to railcars, which ran only as far as Te Puke. The significance of Taneatua died away. The Taneatua Express had enjoyed a reign of over 30 years, ten years longer than its predecessor, the Thames Express. The railcar era ended in 1967, only eight years after its inception.

In 1976 I had a belated chance to travel along the path of the Taneatua Express when an excursion train called the 'Gorges Special' travelled from Auckland via Hamilton, before ending its journey at Mount Maunganui. We enjoyed the delights of the Karangahake and Athenree Gorges and Tauranga Harbour, but unfortunately the train went no further. Certainly not to the mythical Taneatua railhead. Two years later the Kaimai Tunnel, New Zealand's longest, was opened and the old route became redundant.

In 1997 TranzRail ran a railcar service called the Kaimai Express, which operated between Auckland and Tauranga, via the new tunnel. Things were looking up. Perhaps the new powers-that-be would be tempted to extend the service down the matchless, often maritime stretch south of Tauranga, all the way to Taneatua. Failing that, a new scenic service that would surely have had appeal for tourists, could have been introduced to run from Tauranga to the now isolated Taneatua. It would have been the North Island's version of the famed TranzCoastal Express still operating between Picton and Christchurch in the south.

Sadly, such developments never eventuated, and although the occasional excursion train visits the Bay of Plenty, regular passenger services seem a thing of the past. They certainly are along the original route through the gorges, and along the withered arm to Taneatua.

6 Steaming past the mountain

The New Plymouth Express, 1935

The Taranaki region was once a critical cog in the original rail-link between Auckland and Wellington. The line from New Plymouth to Wellington was completed in 1886, long before the main trunk was completed in 1908, and the authorities soon began advertising through services between Auckland and Wellington, utilising existing lines. These included the short branch from Auckland station to Onehunga Wharf and the Taranaki main line. In between there was the small matter of sailing by steamer from Onehunga to New Plymouth, where another train, the Taranaki Express, was waiting.

The journey was a mission. It was almost as if the passengers were off on an overseas cruise as they prepared to board the 'Boat Train' at Auckland Station. Memories were rekindled of English boat trains, where services from London and other cities met cross-channel ferries at Folkestone, Dover and Ipswich. The Onehunga boat train became such an ingrained feature of the Auckland rail scene that even as late as the 1920s, long after the North Island main trunk opened, Newmarket station still boasted the 'Boat Train' on destination hoardings. Such services were so imbued with the romance and wanderlust of an exotic means to reach the capital that Aucklanders were disinclined to let all trace of its existence disappear.

The very notion of trains leading directly to the sea had a particular charm and popularity, even if some of the passengers weren't actually catching a boat. In 1879 the SS *Rotomahana* visited Port Chalmers on her maiden voyage. Two excursion trains were required to cater for those wanting to see the new vessel, and the branch from Dunedin to Port Chalmers hummed with activity. One train was a whopper, with 27 carriages accommodating 2000 passengers. Three years later, a similar train carried patrons from Invercargill down the Bluff line when the SS *Rotomahana* came calling. New Zealand's longest serving boat train, and its most famous, was the Christchurch to Lyttleton service that met the interisland ferry.

While the Onehunga boat train was famous in Auckland, its demise was inevitable when Auckland to Wellington trains began travelling overland all the way on the main trunk.

Previous page

The New Plymouth Express pulled by KA 939 passes Ngaere in 1962.

J.A.T. Terry Photo

Where boat trains used to run. WW678 heads a suburban service to Onehunga through Penrose Junction.

J.A.T. Terry Photo

New Plymouth was a pivotal railway centre when the boat from Onehunga berthed. The line between Marton Junction and New Plymouth was opened in March 1885, 23 years before the main trunk completion. A through service became possible in 1886, once the line of the Wellington and Manawatu Railway, a private company, reached Longburn and the tracks beyond were completed by the government.

By 1901 the train had become a daily service. It was known as the New Plymouth Mail for a time, but gradually, as it sped up, it became the New Plymouth Express, gaining recognition as the longest established New Zealand Railways provincial express. Before the line to Gisborne, on the East Coast, was opened in 1942, it was also our longest running provincial express, in terms of distance.

The mid-1920s were heady days for passenger trains. Roads had yet to develop to a point where the threat of bus and car really impacted. Ten years later services like the New Plymouth Express were still very much part of the landscape and social fabric. A journey from New Plymouth to the capital — and intermediate stops — still saw hundreds utilising the service as the natural way to undertake a long distance jaunt.

On a squally day in 1935, at 8.25am, the New Plymouth Express pulled out of New Plymouth Station. Eight of the very latest wooden mainline carriages — the last to be built — made up the bulk of the train. The new carriages featured such novel developments as roller-bearing bogies, angle iron trusses and a single steel fascia. A faithful AB engine, the force that worked so diligently in the years between 1920 and 1940, was soon spiriting the train along the waterfront and on towards Lepperton Junction. Already the majestic cone of Mount Egmont dominated the landscape. For some passengers the train was known affectionately as the Egmont Express, particularly along the stretch from Inglewood to Hawera.

There's not a lot to see at Lepperton Junction, apart from the beginnings of the branch line to Waitara, part of the first railway built in Taranaki. Although New Plymouth was the dominant settlement, Waitara had the superior port and it made economic sense to link the two. The line was opened in 1875 but lost its significance when New Plymouth developed its extensive breakwater.

Mixed trains served Waitara until 1946, when it became a goods-only line, and as a consequence, very much an afterthought to most. D. B. Leitch, however, in his 1967 publication *Engine Pass,* expressed a contrary opinion at a time when the Waitara line was one of the few to retain steam propulsion.

> The Waitara Shunt lives in a world remote from the rest of New Zealand Railways' system of which it is nominally a part. It carries goods only, knows nothing so regimented as a timetable, and almost without exception runs only during the day — and then only on weekdays. And everyone, from the shunter to the station-master and engine driver, talks about 'Our Train'.
>
> The Waitara Shunt is for me the most fascinating of all New Zealand branch lines.[1]

In 1935, passengers on the express had no reason to contemplate the future circumstances of the Waitara spur — the railways were here to stay. Railway construction was continuing in other parts of the Dominion and besides, there were more important misgivings to occupy the mind, such as the hard times of the Depression, the poor form of the All Blacks in Britain and the fact that Egmont was now partly surrounded in cloud. That meant rain was on the way, although another school of thought held that if you couldn't see Egmont in its entirety, it was already raining, and if you could, it was about to rain.

And who could possibly envisage a time in the far-off future when the Waitara line would be taken over by rail enthusiasts in a preservation capacity? In 1935 there were no rail enthusiasts, just New Zealanders who were enthusiastic about the railways or, at the very least, comfortable with their domination of cross-country travel.

In 1877 construction of the main Taranaki line reached Inglewood, and in 1935 the express passes through around nine. Half an hour later, it's sitting at Stratford Junction while passengers rush for refreshments. It seems a little early in the journey, but the train empties anyway, with some angling for a better view of Egmont from the platform, across the dairying plains. Light rain soon turns into a heavy downpour, although Egmont is still prominent to the west, putting the lie to the notion that if it's raining you can't see the mountain. Or the other way round. Soon you can't see Egmont and the rain stops.

Hacking out the Stratford-Okahukura line at the Huiroa cutting and laying tracks through the wilderness.

HCL-08867

Stratford is worthy of a refreshments stop; it's a genuine working junction, particularly since a year or two back when the Stratford – Okahukura line, the S.O.L., was finally opened. It didn't take long for the authorities to take advantage of the fact that Okahukura branched off the North Island main trunk and now passenger services from as far away as Auckland could gain more direct access to Taranaki and New Plymouth.

In September 1933 night expresses began, with the service operating three days a week. On those occasions the Auckland to Wellington Limited took on an odd appearance. It carried an extra guard's van and additional carriages and until curious observers learned the night express to New Plymouth piggybacked at the rear of the limited, they marvelled at its increased patronage.

At Taumarunui, in the depths of King Country nights the extra guard's van and carriages were spirited away by an AB engine back up the main trunk for 11 km to Okahukura Junction, before plunging into the even more darkened recesses along the new branch to Stratford and then on to New Plymouth.

Taranaki was now alive with expresses and incoming northerners, the more so in holiday periods when a fully fledged separate express ran directly from Okahukura to Stratford, without troubling the shunters at Taumarunui when a connecting service to and from Taumarunui operated. Stratford also saw an additional service to and from Hawera link up with the new night express.

By the time writer J. D. Mahoney travelled on the night train in the early 1950s, J-class engines had superseded the faithful ABs, and the trains ran as separate entities to the Auckland to Wellington Limited. He recalled one stop at Matiere, which reflected the utter remoteness of the line.

> The night was pitch black, and there was not a single light to be seen beyond the station. At one stage I could hear the echoing and spasmodic footsteps of what was probably the porter-in-charge. Everything was quiet in the dark carriage; not even the 'glug-glug' of a steam valve. We stayed there for quite a long time, for reasons which remain a mystery. Certainly no train arrived from the opposite direction to make a crossing. There seemed to be an air of unreality about it, so far as a ride on an express train was concerned.[2]

Prospects were altogether brighter when trains reached Stratford. Indeed, Stratford was once under consideration as the junction for the North Island main trunk, with the line veering through Taranaki, before the central North Island route received the nod. Not surprisingly, Taranaki interests lobbied vigorously for this variation.

In 1879 the first line through Stratford — the New Plymouth to Wanganui link — reached the town, but it is the S.O.L. which lent Stratford its somewhat mythical railway heritage. The last spike on the branch line was hammered home by Prime Minister George Forbes in 1932, after 31 years of earnest construction. When the final tunnel, known as Number 3, was pushed through, a bottle of whisky was consumed by the Mayor of Stratford and members of the work gang, and the empty bottle embedded in the concrete of the tunnel ceiling.

Prior to that politics had produced some bizarre incidents. When a junction was being considered for the S.O.L., two settlements further to the south, Ngaere and Eltham, both entered bids. Prime Minister Richard Seddon, while attending meetings to discuss the issue, was said to have been tripped up and sent sprawling by a rope extended across a darkened aisle at one such meeting in Eltham. Suggestions were made that it was a Stratford rope which had caused King Dick's momentary fall from grace, an act designed to discredit Eltham's claim and turn the PM's favour in Stratford's direction. The latter happened, rope or no rope, and in 1901, when the first sod was turned, Stratford enjoyed a day of prolonged celebrations. According to diarists of the time, everybody was 'full and o'er flowing'.

As the railhead advanced into the backblocks and truncated services started, the line developed a special folklore. Sometime in the 1920s a Tututawa family received a telegram by telephone: 'Mum dead, arriving back at Stratford by train tonight.'

The concerned parties gathered, grieving, at the station. The undertaker was poised with hearse and heavy heart. The train finally pulled in and Mum was the first off the train, very much alive. The message had been misunderstood over the phone and should have conveyed the following information: 'Mum, Dad, arriving back at Stratford by train tonight.'[3]

When the first Taranaki to Auckland express ran though Stratford and on to the S.O.L., several ladies secured the train driver's autograph. Boys put pennies on the line, not in an attempt to derail proceedings, but to secure bent coins with increased currency.

During the 1980s, as passenger services on the line were withdrawn, the Stratford Aero Club raised funds by running successful 'High Country Flyer' round trips from Stratford, along the S.O.L. to the Main Trunk, and back to Taranaki via Marton Junction in the South.

Awareness of the S.O.L.'s unique qualities saw ideas mounted for renewed passenger and excursion trains. To celebrate the dawn of the new millennium in 2000, a proposal that a 'National Parks Express' linking Tongariro, Whanganui and Egmont National Parks, utilising the now forgotten S.O.L., was mooted. Sadly, such a service never saw the light of day. Stratford, although still hosting freight trains, is only visited these days by passenger services in the form of occasional excursion junkets.

As the New Plymouth Express passed through Te Roti Junction in 1935, the Opunake branch headed directly across country towards the Tasman Sea. Passengers were able to travel down the branch to the seaside, where 'Opunake today is a sleepy little town, a holiday resort, famous for a glorious surfing beach.' Joyce West went on to describe the summer scene in Opunake where 'the foaming surf is gay with laughter and shouting and tumbling bronze bodies.'[4]

Less than an hour after its stop at Stratford, passengers were invited to partake of more pies and cups of tea at Hawera. The ocean wasn't far away as the line continued a few miles inland from the South Taranaki Bight. A bite of another kind was offered at Patea too, little more than half an hour after Hawera, with every stop determined to have its slice of the railway pie. Soon the express was working its way beyond the Taranaki Plains and into the hillier regions of Wanganui. Waverley, Waiototara and Westmere slipped past and passengers were beginning to wonder if every settlement in the Wanganui area, both Maori and Pakeha, began with the letter W. They might have also pondered the notion of yet another food stop at Aramoho Junction, after sandwiches in Stratford, ham and mustard in Hawera and pies in Patea.

Aramoho had other diversions — literally. At one time a service known as the 'Taranaki Flyer' linked New Plymouth with Wanganui, via Aramoho, but in 1935 Wanganui was one of the few New Zealand cities not visited directly by a main line. A connecting train, 'The Ferry', waits at the opposite platform to take Wanganui passengers into the heart of the city. The 'musical chairs' performed by the locomotives is both bewildering and diverting. The AB from New Plymouth that has hauled the express thus far is uncoupled and assigned to the short train awaiting to depart for the city, and a Wanganui AB recently arrived at the head of 'The Ferry' now pulls the express.

In earlier times through trains ran unmolested down the Wanganui branch from Aramoho to the central city and back, but the arrangement in 1935 was designed to speed the express on its way. In 1927 a weekend excursion train from Wellington ran directly to Wanganui city station, beyond which the Castlecliff branch carried more modest numbers of excursionists out to the Wanganui River Heads, where they enjoyed fishing, picnicking and swimming. At one time the Castlecliff line supported six daily passenger trains each way, but over the years patronage dwindled and in 1932 passenger services were cancelled.

The 1927 excursion was typical of the type of 'fun' train run by New Zealand Railways during the golden years of passenger travel. Four hundred Wellington excursionists embarked on the journey to Wanganui where the railways, in a package deal, had arranged activities and accommodation. Concession rates were negotiated with Messrs Hatrick and Co., Wanganui riverboat proprietors, who ran the *Waione*, *Ohura* and *Wakopai*. Boat trips up the scenic river were so alluring seats on the train were snapped up and the Department was obliged to close booking facilities long before the train departed the capital. Intense publicity and the promise of low fares and charges guaranteed the success of the venture.

A ghost of the Taranaki Flyer. Revisiting a fine tradition, an excursion train from 1962 – an Anniversary Day special – hurtles along the Wanganui branch line, powered by Ks 912 and 914.

J.A.T. Terry Photo

No fewer than 14 carriages snaked past Aramoho Junction onto the Wanganui branch, and a memorable exploration of the city and its awe-inspiring river. The rallying cry of 'Boys, Boys, Boys!' headed a handbill circulated amongst passengers, advising of a fireworks display (it being 5 November) to be held that night at Cook's Gardens. The Corporation of Wanganui compiled a promotional folder, outlining attractions and events and the Sarjeant Art Gallery, picture theatre, dance halls and supper rooms were all well attended.

The 1927 Wellington to Wanganui excursion was the first such jaunt between the two cities organised by the Railways Department. It was so well received, particularly the boat journeys on the river that had 'made New Zealand famous'— during the course of which a Mr Takarangi pointed out historical features — further excursions were promised. At one stage the three steamers plied the straight reaches where William Webb and Richard Arnst, world-class scullers, practised their craft prior to competing in the world sculling championships.

When in Wanganui, a trip up the river was almost mandatory. Here the twin-screw steamer *Ohura* makes good progress.

ATL-1/1-000489-G

The general expansion of rail services along the Taranaki main line, both regular and excursion, was highlighted in 1939 when the new railcars were introduced. The *Wanganui Herald* described the new craft in glowing tones: 'A silver streak of railway efficiency, Aotea, railcar R.M. 30, cut the Wellington-New Plymouth timetable from nine and a half hours to seven and a half hours.'[5]

Momona Tamihana spoke for the Maori people during the ceremony held at New Plymouth station to inaugurate the new service. He saw the railcar as being the new canoe for the young people, although it should remind them of the old canoe, Aotearoa, which carried the Maori of old to New Zealand. He suggested the railcar should be named Aotearoa, a notion readily taken up by Mr G. H. Mackley, General Manager of Railways. James Cowan, the historian, confirmed that Aotea was the early name of Tahiti, from which Turi, the main ancestor of the Taranaki iwi, had sailed to Taranaki.[6]

In 1935 steam-drawn expresses still ruled the rails. The railcars would encroach more and more on their domain in the years ahead but in 1935 the New Plymouth Express was still a going concern and at around 12.30 it got going out of Aramoho Junction. The AB made good progress, while in a wider sense progress was soon to supplant the ABs. In the late 1930s the massive new K locomotives would make their presence felt on the New Plymouth Express, once the main trunk was encountered at Marton Junction. In the meantime the AB-hauled express pulled into Marton just before two in the afternoon, still entrusted with the train all the way to Wellington.

Inevitably more refreshments were available at Marton, where a fully equipped dining room was operating. The junction settlement was located three kilometres down the road from the town itself, which had been named after Captain James Cook's birthplace in Yorkshire.

The rest of the journey along the North Island main trunk from Marton, through Feilding, Palmerston North, Levin, Otaki, Paraparaumu, Paekakariki and on into Wellington, is part of the story of the Auckland to Wellington Express. In 1935 the New Plymouth Express still approached the capital in spectacular fashion as it drifted down the old Wellington and Manawatu Railway Company's main line, through its sharp reverse curves, the suburban enclaves of Johnsonville, Raroa, Khandallah, Box Hill, Ngaio and Crofton Downs and seven short tunnels, as it skirted the bush-lined Ngaio Gorge. Beyond Crofton Downs the waters of Wellington Harbour glistened, the clock struck 6pm, and passengers readied themselves for disembarkation.

Off to the east the two long tunnels of the new Tawa Deviation, a more practical if less charming manner of approaching the city, were approaching readiness for trains using the main line. When the new Wellington Railway Station was opened in 1937, it also signalled the full commencement of services through the Tawa Deviation, bringing to an end an era in passenger train travel out of the capital.

An excursion train known as the Fields Express to Palmerston North was the last through service to use the old line via Ngaio and Johnsonville.

Before that, the New Plymouth Express pulled out of Wellington not long after ten in the morning, and with two AB engines willing the train over the Hutt Road and up the steep, curving track into the hills, the sound of the engine exhaust reverberated in the northerly. It was regular enough to set your watch by.

Nearly ten hours later the express would be coming off the Taranaki Plains, with Egmont now a retreating shadow, and coasting into New Plymouth Station, over 400 km away.

Many years after the demise of the New Plymouth Express, I set about travelling on the Taranaki lines. In the late 1960s the Wellington to New Plymouth railcar was still running, as was another railcar service through the backblocks along the S.O.L. The latter left at an ungodly hour but it was a novel way to get out of Taranaki, onto the main trunk, and back to my

Trailblazer on the Manawapou Viaduct. In 1939, Aotea, a Standard-type railcar, was the first such vehicle to run along the route of the New Plymouth Express.

J.A.T. Terry Photo

home-base at Te Kuiti. It was a moody, dark passage in the depths of night, quite unlike the sun-drenched, daylight railcar run from Wellington to New Plymouth. I slept a good part of the way, which was disappointing.

A year or so later I had cause to travel on the night railcar again, this time from Te Kuiti to New Plymouth via Taumarunui. I was determined to stay awake this time, if only to see what you couldn't see. It was like a night trip through Siberia — it seemed that cold. The New Plymouth railcar left Taumarunui at another ungodly hour from a dock platform I didn't know existed.

Four fellow passengers climbed aboard, on a Friday night, stepping around a clutch of drunks, one of whom asked me for a dollar to pay for a shot of rum for his poor wife and family. Soon we were swerving and shrilling through the back of beyond; through 24 tunnels you sensed were there because of the change in atmospherics in the carriage and the unpleasant plugging of ears; on through sunken valleys and tight gorges that occasionally revealed themselves as hill-lines momentarily illuminated by rogue moonlight. Lonely homesteads with white-faced facades flashed past. Did anyone live there? Flicks of moving white on hillsides were probably sheep disturbed by the sudden intrusion of a mechanical monster — it was unlikely anything else would be out there.

Occasionally, at places like Ohura and Whangamomona, bright station lights woke sleepers. As the railcar screeched to a halt, a shady figure might alight, another with dour face thrown into ghostly profile by the harsh Colditz-like lights, would clamber noisily aboard, his curse while struggling with the door latch the only human sound encountered at another whistle stop on one of New Zealand's quietest railways.

The blackness continued. The hovering valleys and tunnels intensified. The perpetual dark heightened my desire to travel this route with the sun shining, or at least through the cloud cover and drizzle often encountered in this part of the railway world.

As the line left the hilly clefts of inland Taranaki and straightened out on to the downlands approaching Stratford, the fleeting glimpses of Toko and Douglas receded and smudge of lights signalling larger settlements brought a sense of both reassurance and disappointment. I couldn't wait to tell those interested enough to listen that I had travelled through New Zealand railways' back of beyond. I couldn't say I'd seen much though, given the bleak blackness of night. Until now the line, all 143.49 km of it, had seemed like one long tunnel.

'I travel on the railcar every Friday,' a fellow passenger revealed, telling me her name was Rosemary. She must have been sitting next to me since Ohura or Whangamomona. I had been half sleeping, half ruminating, hard up against the window and totally unaware of her presence. Her voice sounded like a ghost in the night.

'I prefer to travel with company,' she continued. 'It gets a bit freaky along this line.' I admitted to feeling a bit freaked. I couldn't even see her as the railcar continued hammering through the hills. Rosemary's company was appreciated, as she knew a bed and breakfast outfit in New Plymouth that stayed open especially to cater for the handful of passengers arriving on the railcar at around two in the morning.

As the railcar bucked and swayed beyond the Okahukura junction points, I thought of the people to whom this branch line was something of a miracle. The sparsely populated inland Taranaki hills more than qualify as the proverbial back of beyond, yet have a railway running through them. With so many tunnels, twists and turns, it should be decorated as a monument to the golden age of railways and the indomitable spirit of engineers and rail-builders. During the desperate years of the Depression, railway construction camps became established in inhospitable places such as the Tangirakau Gorge, creating a settlement of 1200, a sizeable population. Bob Scott, who became one of New Zealand's best All Blacks, spent part of his boyhood in the camps and settlements that set about opening up the backwater.

The advent of the motorcar and the very nature of the country itself ensured that this corner of New

From the backblocks to the big smoke and All Black fame. The redoubtable Bob Scott in his Petone menswear store, 1956.

ATL-1/2-177093-F

Zealand would never truly be opened up. More land may have been cleared for farming, but there are no cities along the line. Nor are there service towns of the significance of Te Kuiti, Taumarunui and Taihape along the main trunk. Ohura, with its prison, coal mines and farming, became one of the more populous towns on the line, but never truly burgeoned. Whangamomona, towards the Taranaki Plains, also had its moments of influence, but until townsfolk declared it a republic in recent years, few New Zealanders had heard of the place.

Historian James Cowan recalled the time he trudged for days with a railway exploration party through the lonely ramparts and valleys: 'There was not a habitation of man between the upper Ohura and the outskirts of Stratford, a distance of over 80 miles.'[7]

That was back in the late 1890s. Obviously settlements had sprung up somewhere along the line in the following decades, but I wasn't privy to their whereabouts. Writer O. N. Gillespie described an 'enormous mass of mountains and ravine, tumbled plateau and broad valley, bush-clad ridge and hidden swamp.'[8] The railway ran through such physical wonders as well, but because my journeys had been under cover of darkness, I felt deprived.

Eventually, in 1976, I finally saw what O. N. Gillespie described — a true rural rail backwater. The daytime mixed goods train from Taumarunui to Stratford, a slow, meandering all-day affair, enabled a thorough immersion in the physical grandeur and utter remoteness. By the time we reached Whangamomona it was time for reflection.

Sitting on the front veranda of the pub, where we sipped coffee or something stronger, a diesel-drawn freight train rumbled past, going the other way. Right up until the late 1970s, our train, a mixed freight train with a carriage attached to the rear, provided a daylight service. Whangamomona's general store once received visits from people living further inland who would top up their groceries, visit the pub, and travel back on the east-bound complementary service from Stratford. The mixed goods, one of the last such appendages on the S.O.L., was also known as the 'pictures' train. Locals used to ride the rails on a Saturday afternoon all the way to Taumarunui to visit the cinema.

It's hard to believe a tri-weekly night express from New Plymouth to Auckland — originally steam-hauled — used to ghost through here in the past. Fiat railcars replaced the expresses in 1956 and the experience of swishing and swaying though the pitch black backblocks on the night express became part of New Zealand rail folklore.

In 1971 the Auckland to Taumarunui section of the railcar service was terminated and, two years later, daylight services from Taumarunui to New Plymouth were introduced. Local roads, including the Lost World Highway, had been improved by then and the continuation of the passenger service was seen very much as a social concession, not a revenue gatherer. The service took on a Heath Robinson aspect in 1978, when a train made up of a diesel engine continued the link, pulling old railcar shells converted into carriages. In 1983 the last passenger train ran, in January. With little fanfare, and certainly minimal patronage, inland Taranaki was left to its own devices — motorcars and the odd bus.

Captivation is a common condition of travellers stopping off at Whangamomona for a casual coffee — or something stronger. Someone — usually one of the 30 locals — might tell you a story about the hemmed-in little hamlet, which was very much a railway community in the old days. Like the time an inebriated railway worker caught a train with the intention of travelling back to Stratford. After jumping into the guard's van the worker felt the need to 'water the shrubbery' on the side of the track, through the open guard's van door. The train lurched suddenly, pitching the reprobate into the wilderness. Luckily the guard witnessed his unscheduled departure, drew the train to a stop and on realising the worker's bloodied condition, issued the driver with instructions to proceed with all due haste to Stratford, where the hospital would deal with the situation.

On arrival at Stratford Hospital the severely bloodied man did his best to deny he had been drinking, claiming he had simply come off second best with a bunch of blackberry bushes that had hindered his passage onto the train.

My final experience of Taranaki passenger services covered a section of track where passenger trains in the province first began, when in 2005, the Waitara Railway Preservation Society provided the only regular passenger train ride in Taranaki.

The Waitara vintage railway was a time warp: a restored branch line masquerading as a vintage train ride. It meant several things to many people, not that there were a lot of passengers that particular squally morning, with blue patches of sky being overwhelmed by dark grey clouds, full of rain. A couple of boy racers skidded down the main street. The New World supermarket, opposite the train's starting point, catered for dishevelled shoppers in track pants and sleeveless tops who were making do in a small, isolated Taranaki town that had seen its share of heartache and hard times.

Once the Waitara railway is really up and running and a station is installed down by the river, with slinky carriages and a nuggety restored steam engine at the head of the train, the Waitara rail experience may help transform the town.

In the meantime an old diesel built for progress in either direction cranks us along the town flats, and across a couple of road crossings, before climbing like a real train around the fringes of the town.

'Please wave at the old folk in the old folks' home,' the young guy with the microphone at his disposal pleads. We do, but the old folk seem too absorbed in their backgammon and crochet to take much notice. Mt Taranaki — previously known as Egmont — glints through the pine trees, a full cover of winter snow bejewelling the upper reaches. We pass an area which used to be given over to greyhound racing, where special trains once carried punters from the town up the grade to the race track on race days.

One of the interesting features of the Waitara vintage railway is that it could, at a pinch, be switched over to the main Taranaki line as it emerges from its climb into Lepperton. In terms of continuity it would be possible to travel by train down the main line to Stratford where the inland Taranaki

The Waitara Railway Preservation Society train. Taranaki's newest train on the oldest route.

Graham Hutchins

branch hives off to the east, to eventually link with the North Island Main Trunk at Okahukura.

If all the roads in Taranaki were closed, it would be reassuring for the people of Waitara to know they still had access to the rest of the North Island simply because a bunch of enthusiasts had taken the time and trouble to resurrect the old Waitara branch. Fanciful? Undoubtedly. But such a notion became a talking point as the train swayed up the grades, just as it had all those years ago when the line was part of Taranaki's first railway. Those were the days, ten years before the New Plymouth Express first stretched its legs along the main Taranaki line, and they were never better exemplified than in the following extract from the *Poverty Bay Herald,* when the New Plymouth Express was in its prime.

> The express train that left the Wellington-Manawatu station at 8 o'clock on Monday morning was one of the longest that has ever steamed out of the Thorndon Station. Carriages were added until there were twenty-two long carriages, all of which were filled with a gay crowd, bound for

> Wanganui to see the rowing event of the year. So crowded was the train that many had to be content with standing room on the platform, and in many cases two stowed themselves in seats built for one, but nothing mattered much. They were all in great spirits, and plenty of harmless raillery was exchanged. The crowd was brightened by the presence of the Mornington and Woolston brass bands, on their way to the contest at New Plymouth, and Madame Clara Butt, the great vocalist, and her company, were amongst the passengers. People joined the train at nearly every station, and at Palmerston North it was found necessary to add four more carriages. The whole of Palmerston seemed to be on the platform, which presented a lively scene when the record train drew up. The Palmerston North band, which was also proceeding to New Plymouth, played selections in the brilliant sunshine, giving the scene quite a carnival air.[9]

Those were the days!

7 A year before the quake

The Napier Express, 1930

When the line through the Manawatu Gorge was completed in 1891, the first of the Napier – Wellington express trains were able to link up with the tracks of the Wellington and Manawatu Railway — a private company — and continue on to the capital. Six years later, with the completion of the NZR line through the Wairarapa, the Napier – Wellington service was able to utilise an all-government route that saw the train head south of Woodville, through Masterton and other Wairarapa settlements, before tackling the world-famous Rimutaka Incline.

In 1908 the government purchased the Wellington and Manawatu Railway, and from 1909 the Napier Express, initially known as the Napier Mail, was re-routed again through the Manawatu Gorge and Palmerston North and on to the line that was now part of the main trunk. The final passage of the Napier – Wellington train was a far speedier option than that associated with the bottleneck created at the end of the Wairarapa line by the Rimutaka Incline. In 1930, it is the route taken by the Napier Express on a sunny June day.

Around 8.30am the AB-hauled train left Napier Station. Mail bags and luggage were accounted for, and the departure was orderly. Beyond the clenched knot of city backyards, where women tended garden plots, their skirts hitched high in their britches, and old men waved at the train, their briar pipes sending up a complementary blast of tobacco smoke, the AB engine increased its cough of coal exhaust. As the long line of carriages swung along the waterfront, passengers brightened. Seeing the ocean revived memories of holidays at the beach, shellfish plundering, driftwood fires and perhaps a secretive tipple. Sandcastles and paddling in the sea were a reflection of a time when honest, coal-burning steam engines carried holidaymakers to their beach of choice.

Memories were cast even further back to the very early days of the Napier line, when a more leisurely approach to rail operations and timetables prevailed. High speeds were frowned upon. Flat-out, back then, equated

Previous page
The Napier Express nearing Ngaio in 1911.
ATL-APG-1385-1/2-F

to 40 kilometres per hour. The convenience of passengers was paramount. One family lived close to the line near Pakipaki and when they intended travelling by train a chair was placed beside the track to alert the driver, and an unscheduled stop was made.

In 1930 the Napier Express, a more urgent beast, heads inland away from the coast. It would have been more stimulating for the line to carry on round the lip of Hawke Bay, but that would have presented the problem of access south of the vertiginous cliffs of Cape Kidnappers to the plains beyond. Instead the train followed the flat terrain beyond Clive and, by way of compensation, through the rich crop lands and sparkling green paddocks of the Heretaunga Plains.

Hastings, Napier's twin city, arrives in next to no time, less than half an hour down the line. The Napier Express imposes itself on the centre of town with the line accompanying the main street. A huge throng of swirling women in their finery muster their children on to the train while mail attendants and moustachioed station officials oversee the loading of baggage and light goods in the guard's van. The guard oversees the overseers with a series of hand signals and one-word commands. Between the world wars New Zealand is firmly in the grip of a stern, regimented rail system.

Mainly moustachioed and taciturn, railway staff – including the dog – took their jobs seriously.

J.A.T. Terry Collection

As the Napier Express eases out over the plains and into the approaching hills of Hawke's Bay with their golden glow, the number of passengers swells. At Waipawa a flock of farmers bound aboard and several 'knitting nanas' don't drop a stitch. Waipukurau, a refreshment stop, is reached in good enough time for the train to depart at around 10am.

When the line was steadily advancing south, the completion of the Waipukurau railway bridge and the 'grand' opening of the local station in September 1876 was celebrated by an 800-strong crowd. Such events were boisterous and joyous for a scattered, pioneering population, for whom the railway ran like a lighted beacon through their lives.

As the crowded celebration train arrived from Napier a woman ceremonially smashed a bottle of champagne over the steam engine, and a commemorative elm tree was planted at the rear of the station. With the Napier brass band performing the role of Pied Piper, the crowd were coaxed the kilometre or so to the Tavistock Hotel for luncheon. Feasting, largely of a liquid nature, continued all afternoon. On the traipse back to the station the band was less tight musically, although most were tight in another sense. They had lost their pulling power as well, probably because by now each instrumentalist appeared to be calling his own tune.

Despite the vigilance of rail officials more than a handful of revellers missed the train. The beer had gone down well and continued to do so. It was noted at the time that, despite the inconvenience to stranded passengers, they would at least remember the day long after the more sober ones. It was also noted that those still holed up in the Tavistock Hotel would probably remember little.

The guard on the express in 1930 gave the impression of being less tolerant of such aberrant behaviour. A tall, rakish figure with smudged glasses dangling precariously on the tip of his nose, he presented a firm but friendly persona. And despite the occasional jolting and listing of the train and the ever-present jostling of excited passengers, his glasses never left his face.

The express climbed into the hills through Takapau and Kopua. As early as 1879, a year after the link had opened, a section further down the track was witness to an angry Maori chief with a tomahawk and a line blocked by rail sleepers.

The chief was not out to perpetrate New Zealand's own Great Train Robbery — he was looking for retribution. Nominally it was about a tactless Pakeha guard and his inappropriate way of dealing with a Maori passenger who smoked his pipe in a non-smoking area on an earlier train. In a sense it was a red herring. The real issue was the fact that the government had not paid an agreed sum to the chief and his people for the land over which the Hawke's Bay line now ran.

Tohua, the chief protagonist and the one manhandled over the smoking issue, was not out to stop the train travelling through. All he wanted to do was delay it temporarily, seek out the pompous guard and whack him with his tomahawk.

The new technology of the day saved the guard. The railway telegraph carried the message, tapped out urgently to an intermediate station. The intended victim was able to keep his head down, and the incident served instead to highlight the tardy payment system which had upset Tohua.

In another incident a few years later, a firm of railway contractors shot through, owing significant sums in labourers' wages. The workers stormed into the Dannevirke Hotel, took possession of the watering hole and demanded their plight be addressed. Whether or not it was addressed seemed less significant than the rousing of police reinforcements from Napier, who travelled down by a later train to sort out the situation.

The plains have long gone as the train climbs through viaduct country. Kopua (29 m), Ormondville (39 m), Makotuku (26 m), Matamau (30 m), Piripiri (29.5 m), and Mangatera (25 m) carry the line through broken country and the highest point on the journey, at 305 m.

At 11.30 the train reaches Dannevirke, the next stop. The line reached Dannevirke in 1884, after bypassing the disappointed folk of Norsewood, whose village was condemned to a rail-less state as construction gangs forged the line straight through the 70-mile bush from Takapau. Dannevirke nearly missed out — the original intention was to locate the line a kilometre or so from the centre of town. Considerable agitation lead to a change of plans and Dannevirke ended up with its rail connection.

Just on midday the express pulls into Woodville Junction. Time for refreshments and the connection to the Wairarapa branch service for many travellers. The Wairarapa Mail, a notable express in its own right, is waiting at the platform. Midday at Woodville Junction was a lively time, and had been ever since the line opened. On 22 March 1887 hundreds of locals and others from further afield queued around the ticket window to buy passage on a special celebratory train scheduled to head north to Napier for the first time. Close to 1500 passengers took their places on a 19-carriage configuration hauled by three J-class engines.

In 1930 the pandemonium persists. With both the Napier Express and the Wairarapa Mail standing at the station, the refreshment rooms, which were privately operated until 1921, seethed with patrons. Katherine Mansfield, the New Zealand writer, described it as 'a great barn of a place — full of primly papered chandeliers and long tables — decorated with paper flowers — and humanity most painfully in evidence.'[1]

The crowd at Woodville Station thinned out at 12.13pm as the Wairarapa Mail pulled away from the platform, twenty minutes ahead of the Napier Express. Some on the latter no doubt felt a pang of regret at not being on the Wairarapa Mail, one of New Zealand's most distinctive provincial expresses, largely because of the Rimutaka Incline.

To many the Rimutaka Incline was a merry roller-coaster ride and a national treasure, with a surprising reputation in parts of the world where railway lines were thick on the ground. The chortling, smoke-enshrouded little Fell engines, like large black pit ponies, became a familiar sight and sound around the wind-swept bluffs and broom-blown valley walls. Not that many people lived there to see them — the odd farm house in a clearing, served by a tourniquet track on the horizon, or a ganger's hut accessible only by rail, were the only signs of habitation between Cross Creek and Summit.

To others the Rimutaka Incline was an encumbrance — a sooty, wind-ravaged right of way (and rite of passage for those who wished to claim

familiarity with the New Zealand rail system), that had to be borne. If you wanted to escape the hemmed-in capital and travel northeast to the Wairarapa, the incline wasn't so arduous. It was essentially downhill between Summit and Cross Creek, although speed restrictions were still severe and brake wheels screamed. Still, there was no point having a runaway express on your hands, not after the passengers had had their spirits lifted with a cup of tea and pie at the Kaitoke refreshment rooms.

Blackened bludgeons on a railway rite of passage. Fell engines h201 and h203 emerge from Summit tunnel on the Rimutaka Incline.

J.A.T. Terry Photo

The true rite of passage was to be a passenger on the Wairarapa Mail as it angled skyward on the 1 in 15 gradient climb from the Wairarapa to Wellington on the other side of the Rimutaka Ranges. The Fell engines, usually three or four of them, were marshalled at intervals along the line of carriages before setting out on the tortuous incline. Usually the ascent was plain sailing, although sometimes it was a challenge.

Margaret Oborn of Raumati Beach, a passenger familiar with the line, recalls an experience on the Rimutaka Incline:

> Once I was to be greatly anxious when travelling on my own back to Wellington, and the train could not get to the summit. The Fell engines backed down to Featherston from where we were bussed to Wellington. All I could think of was poor Dad pacing the station wondering where I was. I remember a bell ringing as the train got to the top in the middle of a tunnel, the wild wind at Cross Creek, looking out of the window to see the other carriages way behind, arriving filthy dirty from the smoke and soot, and the train being so slow you could get out and walk.

Despite the vicissitudes of the Rimutaka Incline, the passage of the Wairarapa Mail was still appealing. Author H. Hector Bolitho sang its praises:

> From Woodville we passed into the Wairarapa district, a vast agricultural area, wealthy and beautiful. It is girded by towering mountains, snow-capped in winter, and concealing some of the most wonderful scenery in the world.[2]

The townships of Pahiatua, Eketahuna, Mauriceville, Masterton, Carterton and Featherston stud the line, but the most interesting settlement, from a railways perspective, is Woodside Junction. Here the short branch line to Greytown sets out eastwards. In the 1930s regular passenger services operated on the branch in days before car ownership impinged on the importance of the railways.

Margaret Oborn recalls:

> We enjoyed several farm holidays in the Wairarapa in the late 1930s. As we had no car, we used the railway to get from our home in Wellington. We had many relatives in the Wairarapa and stayed either in Masterton or Battersea, just south of Greytown. To access the latter we alighted at Woodside to catch the Greytown train. It was fun catching the one engine, one carriage 'puffer' that met the Wairarapa Mail.

Meanwhile, from Woodville the Napier Express eased its way westwards through the Manawatu Gorge. At 12.50pm it arrived at Palmerston North. Here passengers connecting with the northbound New Plymouth Express changed trains. The Napier Express was now running along the southern reaches of the main trunk and made good time as it headed for the end of the island. The Wairarapa Mail, running down the other side of the ranges, would take five and a half hours to reach Lambton Station, in Wellington, largely because of the Rimutaka Incline. The Napier Express took close to three and a half hours to reach its Thorndon Station terminus in the capital, after ghosting down the hill towards the harbour beyond Johnsonville.

The Napier Express had a reputation for good timekeeping and it was able to pull into the platform a few minutes after 4pm, its scheduled arrival time. The sun was still shining. It had been a long, pleasant and uneventful day. The following year — 1931 — the Napier Express and Napier and its hinterland were visited by an event that still stands as one of the blackest in the country's history.

The Napier earthquake hit at approximately 10.50am on Tuesday, 3 February. Inside eight minutes Railway headquarters was alerted by the stationmaster at Waipukurau that communication to the north had been disrupted. The Napier Express was beyond Takapau at the time, thankfully out of the most seriously affected area. Had its departure time from Napier been later than 8.28am, and in earlier times this had been as late as 10.45am, the result would have been very different.

The viaduct between Ormondville and Kopua was damaged, although this fortunately was discovered before the train came a real cropper. The Napier Express promptly returned north to Takapau. Despite telegraph and telephone poles and other facilities being disrupted, special trains were despatched to the disaster zone with little delay. Food and medical supplies were trained in as far as Waipukurau and lorries carried supplies further north.

The transportation of refugees and casualties from Napier, Hastings and surrounding areas became a pressing commitment. A special hospital train was assembled at Waipukurau and a day after the quake patients left for

Palmerston North. Meanwhile spare carriages and other rolling stock were being rushed in from outlying regions of the North Island, to facilitate the transportation and evacuation of an estimated 20,000 displaced persons. Within 24 hours 150 carriages and 50 wagons were assembled — enough rolling stock, provided capacity loadings were used, to cope with the evacuees.

Repair work on the path of the Napier – Wellington Express continued around the clock and three days after the quake trains could access both Hastings and Napier. When the first refugee train headed south from Napier, with 20 carriages and 1200 passengers, it was a morale-booster for the devastated region. More special trains would follow.

Meanwhile in Moxham Avenue, Hataitai, Wellington, Peg Marshall and her family listened to developments. They were one of the few families in the street to have a radio and it quickly became a beacon for others in the neighbourhood who gathered to keep abreast of the fate of the evacuees and related earthquake events. The radio announcer asked for locals to

What a major earthquake can do to a railway line. The track near Napier after the 1931 upheaval.

ATL-135766-F

come forward if they were able to provide accommodation for refugees arriving by train from ravaged Hawke's Bay. The trains would be pulling into a siding on the wharf at the bottom of Aotea Quay.

Peg and her family went to meet the train, waiting a long time in a queue while officials decided which displaced families would be suitable for those volunteering their services. Peg's father said he could take two adults and two children. They were then assigned a family named Callaghan, consisting of husband, wife and two children. The Callaghans stayed with Peg's family for about six weeks, before deciding to find accommodation in Wellington. They opted not to return to Napier and, with Peg's father's help, resettled in Hataitai, close to their benefactors.

The Dean family of Havelock North also made the choice to relocate. Nora Dean was five years of age when the earthquake hit.

> My mother and we six children, ranging in age from two weeks to seven years, travelled by train from Hastings to Wellington where we caught the express travelling north up the main trunk. At Frankton Junction, Hamilton we caught the Taneatua Express which carried us to Waihi, where we were to live at our Grandma Dean's place in Seddon Avenue.
>
> We had travelled on trains for three or four days straight. Mother had to contend with screaming, frightened children, still suffering from the trauma of the earthquake and the sudden loss of their home.

As the refugee trains tiptoed through devastated Hawke's Bay, evidence of destruction peppered the once placid landscape. Nora's memories of the horrific events and exodus remain fragmentary. Houses sat at crazy angles. Fires burned unattended.

One fellow traveller, in shock or attempting to introduce a certain levity, suggested the quake had shaken the locals out of any complacency. The comment was greeted with silence. The past year had not been an easy one, and there wouldn't have been many feeling complacent. The Great Depression still sat squarely on their shoulders — hundreds were out of work and families struggled. To see the ground buckle and wrench with a sound you would never want to hear again, only seemed to compound the hard times.

The railways were regarded as a saviour, and while at least 256 souls died in the disaster, many families were comforted by the fact that they had escaped with their lives. Eventually life returned to a degree of normality. Special trains were no longer needed, leaving the Hawke's Bay line as the sole preserve of the Napier Express.

Many years later, in easier times, we were lucky enough to travel on the path taken by the Napier Express. In 1967 a railcar travelled from Wellington to Napier via the Rimutaka Tunnel and the Wairarapa. That journey covered the route the Napier Express took during the years 1897 – 1909. Unfortunately we missed out on the Rimutaka Incline, which was superseded in 1955 by the Rimutaka Tunnel. Further railcar journeys saw us travelling up through Manawatu, Palmerston North and the Manawatu Gorge, before linking at Woodville with the Hawke's Bay line. One such journey even went beyond Napier to Gisborne.

In later years designated trains, such as the Endeavour, carried us back over the course of the old Napier Express — the one that took the Manawatu option until its demise. The Bay Express, the final regular service on the route (it ceased running in 2001), was also scheduled to cover the old route. During the course of another rail pilgrimage, at a time when TranzRail had resurrected a number of provincial services in the late 1980s and early 1990s, we took our seats on the new Bay Express. Then fate in the form of a derailment at Otaki played its hand. Two trains — the Bay Express and the northbound Overlander — were stranded in Wellington.

Russell Young recalls:

> After some prolonged head scratching, TranzRail worked out that the Bay Express and Overlander could be combined before travelling up the Wairarapa line to Woodville, rather than going via Otaki to Palmerston

North. As I had never done this trip by rail before I was more than happy with the reschedule, and about one hour behind time we set off. By this time TranzRail staff had come into their own, literally going the extra mile to please the passengers. An unscheduled stop at Featherston, waiting for a southbound goods, ended up with everyone wandering outside in the late morning sun, taking photographs of acres of ballast and bare tracks. The staff were still going the extra mile, lining up Japanese and photographing them. I photograph the guard photographing the Japanese, and everyone is happy. In some ways this unique unscheduled stop on the gravel outside Featherston summed up the mood of the whole trip: the urgency of life in the nineties has gone, moments wait for you to discover and enjoy them. No one has a transistor radio tuned in to the stock market reports, cellphones are silent, no one is pining for Sky Television.

After the Wairarapa there followed a workman-like traverse up a steady incline through narrow sheep-studded valleys towards Woodville. Here the Overlander section of the train was split off and the Bay Express became the Bay Express, as we resumed towards Napier. You become aware that the train is determined to reach the sea, and each valley with its spectacular sharp hills becomes wider as the Express picks up speed. After Hastings, where most of the remaining passengers melt away, there are reassuring views of the Pacific drawing in from our right, signalling completion of our journey.

The same vistas would have greeted travellers on the old Napier Express, although the drift of engine smoke would have made for a less unencumbered outlook.

8 South for the summer

The South Island Express, 1926

In 1997 we travelled on the Southerner, along the route of the old South Island Express. We had travelled long and hard in the previous days to get to Christchurch and the Southerner, covering a massive distance from Christchurch to Invercargill, seemed doubly daunting. Travel weariness and the promise of a winter storm made us edgy.

Russell, my travelling companion, scribbled in his diary:

> The next day is the big one, the Southerner all the way to Invercargill. We approach it as one may a vital rugby match, getting psyched up, shadow punching at the hotel windows and doors, avoiding each other's glances. The taxi arrives early and collapses the building tension, which is eased further by being deposited at a cold Addington Station half an hour before time. The carriage is nowhere near full, a feeling of anticlimax prevails. Just as we are about to pull out our spirits are lifted. Two or three suitcases are flung aboard the carriage from a distance, followed shortly by a breathless, bespectacled student wreathed in woollen clothing, her breath condensing in the freezing outside air. Shambling into our carriage looking in the direction of our seat numbers, until one of us says, 'Is this you here?'
>
> She says, 'Yep, this is me here!' It is difficult to track the following few hours, as they passed so rapidly yet so vividly. Our breathless bespectacled travelling companion was a breath of fresh air. Conversation bubbled and flowed. Our travel weariness dissipated.

In 1997 the spirit of the South Island Express was alive and well. Said to be the friendliest long-distance service in New Zealand, it wasn't just because it travelled the furthest in daylight, it was also a tribute to southern hospitality. On Auckland – Wellington night trains it was hard to get to know your travelling mates when everyone was either asleep, trying to get to sleep, or grumpy because of too little sleep.

You'd have thought that once the first night express was introduced on the South Island route in 1928, broken sleep may have led to a loss of graciousness. But the southern authorities had gone the extra mile to assist with passenger comfort. The overnight train may have reached Dunedin at

Opposite

The South Island Express that plied the line between Christchurch and Invercargill is seen leaving Dunedin behind engine number JA 1241.

J.A.T. Terry Photo

a taciturn time — 6.20am — but because the sleeping cars were shunted onto a quiet siding where Dunedin passengers could snooze until 8am (while the rest of the train thundered off to Invercargill), general goodwill prevailed.

By 2002 the Southerner daylight passenger train between Christchurch and Invercargill ran no more, deemed a failure through dwindling patronage and corporate imperatives. Those New Zealanders old enough to recall the South Island Express were flabbergasted. Although freight trains and the occasional excursion junket continued to operate, New Zealand's first main trunk was no longer graced by a regular, long-distance passenger train. It was tantamount to treason, and a crime against the state when the government of the day turned its back on the Southerner.

The South Island's largest cities, Christchurch and Dunedin, were no longer served by a rail passenger service. Invercargill, in the deep south, was similarly affected. A vital part of New Zealand history was derailed and dishonoured.

The completed link was opened in 1878, and as far back as 1879 the first through-train from Christchurch to Invercargill via Dunedin began operations. The first through-express did not run until 1904, although it began four years before the North Island main trunk was even completed. In terms of the country's rail history the route of the South Island Express was positively ancient.

At the time of the New Zealand and South Seas Exhibition at Dunedin in 1925–26, the country's last international exhibition, the South Island Express was in its heyday. Increased patronage saw the train bulging at the seams, both the southern run between Christchurch and Invercargill and her sister train running from Invercargill towards the north. Christchurch station seethed with exhibition goers, as well as those for whom train travel was standard fare.

The express left from Christchurch's second station — the first had been erected to serve the broad-gauge route to Ferrymead. In 1877 the station site was moved to Moorhouse Avenue to better serve the central business area. By 1926, nearly 50 years on, the Moorhouse Station throbbed with activity and excitement. Not only was the South Island Express set to depart, but boat train and suburban services from the port of Lyttleton, subsidiary passenger trains to Dunedin and other suburban jaunts to Rangiora added to the mix. Since 1923 when the Otira Tunnel was finally opened, linking Christchurch with the Coast, the West Coast Express had increased the rail congestion.

For rail fans and small boys, Christchurch Station was a wondrous place, even if you weren't travelling on any of the departing trains. As well as the expresses, boat trains and suburbans, there were the rural branch-line passenger trains coming and going on the Southbridge, Little River and north line or Cheviot branch to the then railhead at Parnassus. Christchurch was unique in this sense, the only one of the three main city centres to also serve as the terminus for middle-distance trains.

One particular service that excited special interest was the recently installed railcar to Little River. Amidst the steam-driven yeomen of the Christchurch fleet the shiny, Edison battery electric railcar stood out because of its stately, smokeless presence. If the steam engines seemed like

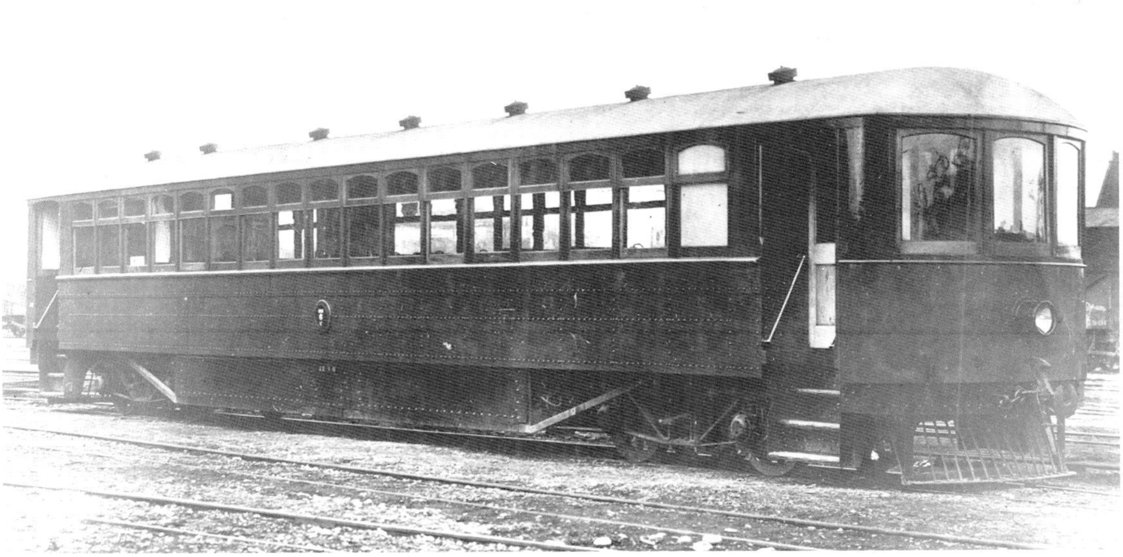

High tech for the times or simply a ghost in the machine? The Edison storage battery railcar in 1926.

ATL-PA1-q-101-091

noisy, playful puppies as they spewed coal smoke into the crisp air and bothersome steam billowed into the path of hurrying passengers, the Little River railcar throbbed quietly like a purring, unobtrusive cat.

Some travellers took such a shine to the railcar they assembled at the station purely to take a ride on the new curiosity. Others, retirees and the well-off, simply had the time and ability to pay the fare. A railway novelty, where trains in general were largely utilitarian and continued to strive for improved timekeeping and comfort, captured the imagination.

As steam-hauled services continued to arrive and depart, with alighting and outward-bound passengers building up their own head of steam, the Little River railcar ran through its departure procedure with a welcome decorum. The journey was more about the means of travel for some, a railcar instead of a blustery, steam-based means of propulsion. Through Hornby Junction, where the Southbridge and Little River services quit the main line, the railcar swayed genially. Prebbleton and Ladbrooks came and went and then, at Lincoln Junction, the Little River branch was left to its own devices. That was another fascination of the journey. A branch line off a branch line. Conventional, steam-hammering services still headed southwest to Southbridge, a ho-hum rural terminus, but the Little River branch held its own secrets.

The railcar passed Greenpark and Motukarara and now there was the spectacular view of massive Lake Ellesmere, as the railcar continued to purr. Kaituna, a stop on the very fringes of the lake, induced superlatives from first-time passengers. One gentleman wanted to alight spontaneously and go fishing, but his wife put paid to such impetuosity. Birdlings Flat saw the line angle sharply, to negotiate the waters of Lake Forsyth, where the same gentleman again expressed a desire to go fishing. Lake Ellesmere might have appeared impressive, but the waters of Lake Forsyth seemed almost overbearing. The lake lapped virtually at eye level as the railcar skirted the expanse and pulled effortlessly into the Little River terminus.

Back at Christchurch Station, if you did have a ticket to ride, a certain amount of concentration was required to ensure you caught the right train. At seven in the morning passengers for the South Island Express, some of whom were no doubt still waking up, had cause to be doubly vigilant. Some visited the refreshment room for an eye-opening cup of tea or coffee. Here passengers off the Lyttleton boat train were being treated to a full, sit-down breakfast after a night on the high seas aboard the steamer from Wellington. It had been a rough passage and some approached their bacon and eggs gingerly. Others could barely keep their eyes open, such had been the disruption to a good night's sleep.

Two AB engines drew the express away from the human maelstrom at Moorhouse Avenue. Today's train was a long one, with extra carriages accommodating the hundreds destined for Dunedin and the Exhibition. With a certain relief passengers settled into allocated seats as the train gathered speed through Middleton, Sockburn (with its short junction line to Riccarton Racecourse), Hornby and Islington. Industrial installations, fertiliser and chemical works and the like presented a grubby visage but soon, as the train headed towards the south after steaming due west for a disconcerting distance, first-time travellers felt more assured that they were on the right train.

At Rolleston, the line to the West Coast branches off, heading for the snow-capped Southern Alps. A bright, clear day lifts spirits, particularly for those passengers who have endured the rough, sleepless steamer crossing, the mad scramble for seats on the boat-train and the grumpy ticket-clipping guard with his offhand demeanour and ghostly lantern while the train was negotiating the long Lyttleton Tunnel. Now as morning light fills the carriage fellow travellers form vivid outlines.

Many women passengers are dressed to the nines. Influences of the Roaring 20s continue to impact. Fashionable shorter skirts and jumpers worn with low belts are an agreeable improvement for those who recall the more voluminous and space-invading styles of earlier decades. Shorter bobbed hairstyles, often topped with 'sensible' hats, seemed to be as perfectly designed for easier passage in the often confined spaces of railway carriages as they are for fashion. Gone are the days of ridiculously large hats surmounting small mountains of piled-up hair, the hats surmounted in turn by flowers, fruit and even feathers.

Some women, blithely unaware of or unconcerned about their view-obscuring headgear, often saw the beginnings, at least, of a train journey as an opportunity to show off such finery. Eventually a long-sufferer, miffed at missing out on the passing scenery, would request the hats be removed, quite an undertaking in itself. Elaborate hat pins with decorative adornments often secured the monstrosity and their extraction was a mission. More than that, hat pins became such a dangerous nuisance on public transport, including trains, that most city and town councils banned them.

By 1926 times had changed. The view from the carriage window of the South Island Express was largely unencumbered, and no one had an eye gouged out by a hat pin as they clambered towards the refreshment rooms. Yet there remained 'fashion' problems for those women who favoured the new high Louis XV heels on their shoes. Surefootedness was often a prerequisite while negotiating the carriage aisle and certainly while joining the refreshment stampede. One wonders how the winner of the first-ever Miss New Zealand contest fared in the 1920s, when she travelled on the express.

As the South Island Express sped across the Canterbury Plains the issue of 'ladies' cars' became pertinent once more. Back in the 1880s ladies' cars had been attached to the Christchurch – Dunedin Express, in response to the threat of annoyance and worse, from often drunken male passengers. They were soon withdrawn, but as New Zealand developed a boozy reputation in the years before World War I, and with the prodding of pressure groups like the Women's Christian Temperance Union, separate train accommodation for women and children again became an issue and in 1919 ladies' cars returned to the South Island Express. In 1926 the ladies' car was still available on the express, but patronage had fallen away. By 1929 the special cars were once again removed.

An old gent suggested, mischievously, that perhaps the ladies' car served a purpose in the era of elaborate but annoying women's hats. They could prod one another with hat pins and have their own vision obscured, in the comfort and confines of their very own carriage.

In the wider world, the train eased to cross the Rakaia River on New

Zealand's longest railway bridge — all 1744 m of it. Rakaia township was the junction point for the Methven branch and where a handful of passengers alighted. Then it was on to Chertsey and Dromore, before the train prepared to enter Ashburton, the first of the refreshment stops.

A father told his son about a terrible train smash that had happened in Rakaia in 1899, causing chaos in the extreme. Four travellers were killed and 40 injured when one excursion train crashed into another, waiting to depart Rakaia Station. The son squirmed in his seat and a matron, overhearing the conversation, suggested the father had chosen the wrong moment to give his offspring a potted history lesson.

Passengers had marvelled at the comfortable camber of the train as it continued to speed across the plains. Mount Cook, New Zealand's highest, had been singled out among the towering peaks of the Southern Alps. Such sights whetted the appetite and most travellers joined the rush to the Ashburton refreshment room.

Still the train hugged the plains and the thought was expressed that soon, surely, the ocean would appear. In contrary fashion the line arced further inland beyond Hinds, before crossing the Rangitata, another of Canterbury's wide and distinctively braided rivers. Temuka and the Opihi River came and went — and Washdyke, where the branch to inland Fairlie curved northwestward — before the express rounded a curve to the Pacific coast. The town of Timaru, and Caroline Bay, were only minutes away.

The Fairlie branch may have presented an inconsequential air, but it boasted a famous train — the Fairlie Flyer. It was perhaps the most notable passenger train to ply the Canterbury branch lines and in 1926 it still attracted a healthy smattering of travellers bound for inland settlements, such as Pleasant Point, Albury and Fairlie itself. Several express passengers intended making the connection with the 'Flyer', a train not outstandingly fast despite its name, but which garnered a healthy popularity because of its ability to bind a community together. It was like a faithful old friend, and sadly, like friends who become infirm with age, in 1926 it was on its last legs. Four years later its days were up and it was superseded by a more utilitarian mixed train.

Essentially the Flyer and the Fairlie branch set out to serve sheep farmers of the MacKenzie Country. In 1914 there were plans to construct extensions all the way to Lake Tekapo, but wartime belt-tightening left the branch languishing in no-man's land — or to be precise, Eversley — a short distance beyond the effective railhead of Fairlie.

Many southern travellers were holidaymakers, honing in on Caroline Bay as the ideal beach resort. In summer it was a Mecca for sun-worshippers and swimmers; in winter, a place of salty contemplation away from built-up city and suburb, and landlocked towns and farms far from the ocean. By 1926 New Zealanders had thrown off the shackles of a restrictive era regarding swimming. At the turn of the century swimming and sunbathing were not popular pastimes, but as the 20th century advanced more and more adults ventured into the waters of Caroline Bay and other beaches, with the sexes rigorously segregated. The practice of mixed bathing was a burning issue but gradually common sense, that good old Kiwi yardstick, prevailed — although the need for 'decency' prompted the Auckland City Council to pass a by-law stipulating that all persons were obliged to wear a neck-to-knee bathing costume.

Swimmers, sunbathers and picnickers dotted the beach at Caroline Bay as the train edged past. Following further refreshments at Timaru the train continued on for some distance, with the sea close at hand, until beyond St. Andrews it headed inland again, through Studholme Junction where the Waimate branch met up with the main line, across the Waitaki River and past the distinctive stone buildings of Oamaru.

Oamaru was also distinctive for rail-related reasons. In 1926 there was no impediment to through travel but, in earlier times, its first station was built in such an awkward location that trains passing through the town could only do so by reversing away from the platform and back onto the main line. It was also the terminus for trains coming off the Tokarahi, Kurow and Ngapara branches.

In 1926 passengers could avail themselves of a swept-up, sit-down meal at the Oamaru Station dining rooms. Sir George Troup had designed

JA 1249 works hard to haul a train out of Dunedin in 1950.

J.A.T. Terry Photo

the stately wooden station, which was long enough to accommodate the elegant dining facility. It was regarded as the most famous of several such installations on the New Zealand rail network, and quite a drawcard.

A 23-minute stop allowed 250 diners to partake of a meal of the highest quality. Second sittings were not unknown and on such occasions the express was delayed until all were replete. Stewed tripe and oysters, and smoked fish with butter sauce (for more conservative stomachs) were some of the culinary delights presented.

A year or two later the captain of the Australian cricket team, during the course of a New Zealand tour, had occasion to praise the fare at Oamaru Station very favourably indeed. It wasn't just a matter of quality either, as in 1926, during the first months of the Exhibition in Dunedin, in excess of 5000 passengers took advantage of meal stops at Oamaru Station in a single day. Admittedly that figure was achieved during the Easter break, but Oamaru Station had a reputation as one of the brightest jewels in the crown of New Zealand Railways.

Amidst the swirl of passengers, locals often took up station at the station in the hope of identifying a familiar face. The South Island Express, like its equivalent on the North Island main trunk, would often reveal sporting heroes, well-known if less admired politicians and even the occasional entertainer, both foreign and local.

In 1903, Dame Nellie Melba, the famous Australian opera soprano, was sighted. 'Madame Melba arrived by express tonight,' wrote the United Press Association. 'Although the weather was wet, a large crowd assembled outside the station. The diva was formally welcomed by the Mayor and Councillors and presented with a bouquet by the Mayoress.'[1]

Such train-traveller spotting was part of the romance of the rails, so aptly identified by historian James Cowan in his booklet celebrating the history and scenic highlights of the South Island main trunk, and trains like the South Island Express.

James Cowan's words took on a more lurid twist in 1908 when the guard on the express came upon a couple copulating in a birdcage compartment. These were no romantic love birds, in one possible interpretation of James Cowan's slogan. These were lewd show-offs who consummated their passion in full view of fellow passengers — and officials — who happened along. The couple maintained their compromising position when the guard approached and from a prone position the man casually handed over their tickets.

Such incidents were rare, although it was not unknown for similar activities to occur in cramped toilets, tunnels (the longer ones presented more possibilities) or under the cover of blankets, greatcoats and darkness.

An elderly gentleman, rugged up against the wind, recalled the time in 1886 that Admiral Tyron travelled on the South Island Express. He may have been a notable and admired fellow traveller in 1886 but in 1893, while sailing between Beirut and Tripoli on manoeuvres, the admiral issued a signal that was misinterpreted by HMS *Camperdown*, causing the latter to ram HMS *Victoria*. *Victoria*, symbol of a glorious age, went down and the lives of the admiral, 22 officers and 336 men were snuffed out.

Following the substantial fare at Oamaru there was little surprise when quite a number of passengers slept through Makeno, Waimotu and Herbert, inland locations, until the train pulled into a rather lonely outpost called Waianakarua. Passengers unfamiliar with the workings of the line expressed surprise, turning to mild concern, when the train appeared to be overstaying its welcome. Hardened travellers recognised this as the location where the southbound express and its northbound equivalent crossed. The express from Christchurch held the main line while the train from Invercargill eased into the loop. Faces flashed past. Some looked vaguely familiar. Others had a hungry set to their mouths. No doubt the anticipation of a substantial repast further up the track at Oamaru was now uppermost in their minds. For what seemed like a split second the tiny hamlet of Waianakarua was visited by 600 strangers as the two trains crossed.

Beyond Hampden, the Pacific Ocean, a mottled blue-green expanse, caused considerable interest. Those seated on the seaward side of the carriage were viewed with envy. Off in the distance Port Moeraki jutted out in the afternoon haze. The ocean-edged aspect of the train's path, over which historian James Cowan had enthused, became apparent. Between Katiki and Shag Point the wide expanse of Katiki Beach, as calm as a millpond today, prompted those leaving the train at Palmerston to make ready for fun in the sun. In 1926, with improving fortunes, many New Zealanders could now afford to take extended holidays, and in the Kiwi scheme of things this often meant several days at beaches like Katiki.

South of Palmerston the locality of Goodwood has tongues wagging. This was the spot, in August of 1878, and now almost sacred in a railway sense, where the final spike was driven to signify the completion of the Christchurch to Dunedin line. That had been nearly 50 years ago, a fact that seemed almost as amazing as the nondescript nature of Goodwood, a windswept outpost.

Waikouaiti, or what remains of it, is the oldest European settlement in Otago, and was once the province's principal port. Boats utilised the Waikouaiti River Estuary for anchorage before heading out to sea at Waikouaiti Bay. All of this history and water-borne significance is hard to fathom now. Waikouaiti settlement seems a little too far inland, although there is estuarine and marshy evidence, and once the train heads south all the pieces fall into place. As it climbs the express reveals the expanse of Waikouaiti Bay and the pristine sands of Karitane Beach. The ocean dominates as the train straddles the green slopes leading to Seacliff, a place of both happiness and sadness. People still flock to the beaches along these reaches, although in 1926 there is more evidence of travellers spending extended holidays. In earlier days of the southern rail route, day excursions carried large numbers to Seacliff, and, closer to the city, Waitati and Warrington. Seacliff is also the location of a mental hospital, a sobering sight as it stands watch on the hill overlooking the bright and breezy Pacific.

From Warrington the engine attacks the precipitous climb around the fringes of Blueskin Bay. The marvels of railway engineering are obvious as the train tiptoes along a virtual cliff face with waving holidaymakers, like ants, looking up from the fringe of a white-sand beach below. Purakanui and, off in the distance, the mouth of Otago Harbour, glisten in the afternoon light before the train disappears into the Mihiwaka Tunnel.

As the express skirted the suburb of Port Chalmers, an old man could be seen fidgeting with a flask. Passengers sharing the seat enclosure either looked askance or looked away. Even the old man's avowal that he was simply plying his poor system with cough medicine did not allay the disgust of a matron at the window seat. The old man barked out an obligatory cough or two to prove his condition, before taking a generous slug of whisky.

The matron harboured memories and grudges of the dreadful suburban service that ran to Port Chalmers from the Dunedin city terminus. It became notorious after Port Chalmers went 'dry' in 1902, when the temperance and prohibition movement did its righteous best to rid the Dominion of the demon drink. Typically it produced the opposite effect. The thirsty sailors and wharfies of Port Chalmers were not to be denied their tipple, and much alcoholic beverage was imbibed at the Dunedin Station bar after the pubs had closed. Just as much seemed to be sloshed and tipped over (perhaps that's how the term tipple emerged) as stumbling passengers poured out onto the platform at closing time.

Refreshment rooms like the one at Dunedin, which served fermented fare, were exempt from the restrictive licensing laws of the day. Inevitably already tanked-up patrons, who continued to drink for the hour and a half extension granted to refreshment rooms, made dishevelled departures when the train summoned them in the dead of night. The late Port Chalmers

train became known as the 'drunkest train in Australasia' and gloried in the name, 'Royal Soaks Express'. It was good for the colonial heart to see the royal connection, less edifying to contemplate the colonial liver being so maltreated.

A Port Chalmers service departs Dunedin in 1946, travelling along the route of the 'Royal Soaks Express'. A lot of whisky was spilt and soaked in the 'auld days'.

J.A.T. Terry Photo

By the time the 1926 express came through, the Port Chalmers train had been sobered up by the actions of Railways Minister Joseph Ward, who banned the sale of liquor at all New Zealand railway refreshment rooms.

Thoughts of such earlier shenanigans recede as the express, having skirted a goodly portion of Otago Harbour, draws into Dunedin's magnificent station, which has served the train since 1907, when it was opened. It is hard to contemplate such a shambles of a train as the Royal Soaks being dispatched from such stately chambers. It is surely the Dominion's most regal rail edifice and a great credit to designer Sir George Troup. A lot of it was Otago's own work, with the main body of the station fashioned out of rock sourced at Hyde in Central Otago. The stone trimmings came from Oamaru.

Those alighting at Dunedin, many to see the exhibition, looked upon Dunedin Station as an exhibition in itself, with mosaic floors and porcelain squares depicting New Zealand rail features. Its very Edwardian grandeur in the heart of the Edinburgh of the South does Dunedin proud. As contingents of exhibition-goers departed for Logan Park, where they would encounter seven exhibition pavilions covering over six hectares, through-travellers felt pangs of jealousy. They would miss out on a grand display that included, as a rail-related aside, the New Zealand Railways exhibit and its centrepiece, steam engine AB608. The latter had been named 'Passchendaele' to honour those members of the department who had lost their lives in World War I, and a year later it would be commissioned to pull the royal train carrying the Duke and Duchess of York around the South Island. It was an engine of some significance.

Meanwhile the working ABs of the express pulled the train away from the excitement of Dunedin minus the retinue of exhibition-goers who would soon contribute to the nearly three and a quarter million visitors who attended the extravaganza in its six months of operation.

As the train eases its way through the southern suburbs calm descends, although those travellers who joined the train at Dunedin are animated enough. A certain travel weariness affects others. It has already been a long day. Christchurch to Dunedin always seemed a significant stretch in itself, but now the final third of the journey to the deep south looms. The invigorating seascapes have disappeared, although when the shores of Lake Waihola appear off to the west, many rouse from their torpor. Wingatui, junction point for the Central Otago line, has been passed in a blur, but now as the line reaches Clarendon, talk of Minnie Dean emerges in hushed corners.

Minnie Dean, New Zealand's infamous 'baby farmer', had been convicted in 1895 of taking the lives of an uncertain number of children and infants. She subsequently became the only New Zealand woman to die on the gallows — the country's preferred method of execution. One of her victims had come from Clarendon and such was the furore created by the case that the mere mention of this rather obscure placename set tongues wagging.

Although the horrific affair occurred all of 30 years earlier, the arrival at Clarendon Station, where an infant Eva Hornby had been uplifted by

Minnie Dean, rekindled unsettling emotions. Eva Hornby's name, over the years, had come to be associated with the South Otago whistle stop.

An association between Minnie Dean and the rail network of Otago – Southland had long been established. She travelled on trains throughout the region in the course of undertaking her dastardly deeds. An observant railway guard at Lumsden, the junction point of the Kingston and Waimea Plains branches, had seen Dean board a train carrying a hat box and a baby. Further down the line near her home at Winton she was observed leaving the train carrying only the hat box. The guard noticed the hat box was unexpectedly heavy as he helped Dean lift it off the train. She was to claim the baby had tumbled off a ledge at Clarendon Station and did not survive the fall. Minnie Dean became infamous as much for the way she blithely travelled in a crowded carriage with a dead baby in a hat box, as for her other abhorrent actions.

After the sobering memories of Clarendon the express reached Milton and Clarksville, where on 19 April 1928, the Roxburgh branch would open for business. At Balclutha the mighty Clutha River, New Zealand's largest in volume, was crossed and the line set out on a distinctly westward course. Since 1915, Balclutha had also been the junction for the Catlins River branch. It had been a long time coming. All of 30 years passed between the time the first section was completed and the final spike hammered home. A. H. McLintock, the historian, had described the Catlins area as being unattractive in terms of likely settlement, the roads all but impassable because of their muddy surfaces. Despite that, the area's potential for forestry was recognised and the Catlins railway forged ahead. Then, in 1904, Premier Richard Seddon visited the Catlins with the news that funds had dried up, unlike the roads, and the continuation of the line to Tahakopa in the forest heartland could not be justified. Times change, and politicians, and 11 years later the line reached its final strategic terminus at Tahakopa.

The long day was weighing down on passengers, but Gore represented a change in mood. As the line followed the course of the Mataura River almost due south again, the end of the island could at least be envisaged.

It was in Gore that the South Island Railway Commissioner, William Conyers, was indeed gored, after a fashion, when he managed to lean so far out of the engine cab his head came into painful contact with a water tank. The accident occurred way back in 1879 during the passage of the first train from Christchurch to Invercargill. Although Conyers survived, he was unable to work again.

The Waimea Plains railway, over which the original Kingston Flyer flew, had branched off at Gore and at Edendale, the short spur through Wyndham to Glenham. Away in the hills to the west, whisky stills were gurgling. According to one gentleman, those were the Hokonui Hills where illicit whisky was distilled, and the source of such exotic firewater could be accessed by rail. They would soon be stopping at a station where, if you played your cards right, a bottle or two could be smuggled on board. Another gentleman scoffed.

It was true there was a tiny station called Hokonui, but it was located a fair way from the Hokonui Hills. And besides, it was a feature of an inconsequential branch that arced away from the Kingston line, a considerable distance from the main trunk. Furthermore it was not, as the first gentleman then suggested, a branch developed expressly to inveigle the whisky out of the district, but a more utilitarian railway that, amongst other functions, served the Hokonui Coal Company. There was no 'whisky train', trumpeted the second gentleman. Perhaps the first gentleman had exhausted his hip flask supplies and was seeking a top-up of the very substance that had rather addled his comprehension of the geography of Southland? This merry exchange created a diversion between Morton Mains and Woodlands. Soon, as the long day dimmed, the outer suburbs of Invercargill signalled the imminent end of the journey.

Invercargill, after all the huffing and puffing, swaying and screeching, nibbling and snoozing, and swigging and snoring, saw the express pull triumphantly into the station three and a half minutes behind schedule. Northerners, who had endured a rough crossing from Wellington to Lyttelton, and a twelve-hour journey from New Zealand's garden city to the deep south, climbed down expecting a polar blast. Instead, as so often happened, the air was still and the temperature seemed no more debilitating than that of Christchurch in the early morning.

Invercargill Station was a modest structure compared to the huge edifice at Christchurch and Sir George Troup's overpowering work of art at Dunedin. The thought was expressed that the ultimate terminus of any famous, long-distance train should be a grand, all-encompassing, end-of-the-line sarcophagus with little indication that the line went anywhere else — a substantial dot on the landscape, a full stop to a Herculean rail odyssey.

Invercargill, however, also provided feeder services. Even as the travel-scarred scurried to uplift luggage, a train going further south to the very end of the island waited. It was a sobering notion to those travellers who saw their grand entry and disembarkation at Invercargill as a defining, and concluding moment. Yet the train to Bluff, even further south again, puffed impatiently. The man with the 'cough mixture' and questionable cough made his faltering way to the Bluff platform. After climbing on board, and draining the hip flask, he was all set for the journey to where New Zealand ended. His inebriated state made it unlikely that he would be visited by sobering memories of the two drunks who managed to fall off this service in 1904, killing themselves in the process.

Mark Twain, the American author, travelled on our trains in earlier times. He seemed to like what he saw.

ATL-037422-F

The preponderance of whisky tipplers in this part of the country was particularly apt because of the deep south's Scottish heritage. There were other British influences of course, and Mark Twain, the famous American writer who travelled on the Invercargill to Bluff service during his journey through various regions of New Zealand, noted in his travel diary: 'A passenger reminds me that I am in "the England of the Far South". ' Such a statement would have been an attempt to convince the author of *Huckleberry Finn* and *Tom Sawyer* that a certain mother-country decorum and respectability prevailed in the rough-edged colony.[2]

The South Island Express, though, kept its worthy reputation intact. Despite the odd tippler, most travellers enjoyed the historic ride in sober but high-spirited fashion. Henrik Van Loon, another American writer, might have later roundly criticised New Zealand's refreshment rooms during the course of his train travels, but in 1926 most passengers could find no fault with the nourishment and service along the route of the South Island Express. Perhaps Mr Van Loon had been asleep when the train stopped at the elegant Oamaru dining facility, or were his observations based on the admittedly deteriorating conditions of future decades?

It could also be added that a year later, in 1927, Ignace Paderewski, the world-famous Polish pianist, highly commended the service provided by New Zealand Railways. It would have to be mentioned that Paderewski, his wife and the pianist's personal representative and business agent were allocated their own designated carriage, which was attached to various services. The route of the South Island Express was one such service and the train's ease of passage, which highlighted scenic wonders such as the Southern Alps, was lauded.

A very important passenger: Ignace Paderewski, the famous Polish pianist. We even treated his pianos with respect.

ATL-098859-F

'You have not a place that is not beautiful,' announced Mr Gordon Joubert, Paderewski's business agent, when he and personal representative Mr Sharp called at New Zealand Railways headquarters. They had come to express gratitude at the outstanding travel arrangements made on behalf of Paderewski and his retinue. Special mention was made of the excellence of the South Island carriage — and the paradisaical country it travelled through. The people were cultured and friendly and even Paderewski's pianos were treated with professionalism and respect.[3]

Had Paderewski and his people travelled in a regular, well-patronised carriage on the South Island Express they would have found the arrangement scarcely less agreeable. Fellow passengers would have been cultured and friendly and if they had felt a little awestruck by their famous travelling companion, they would have carried on regardless, just like the South Island Express itself.

9 Buller or bust

The Nelson Express, 1926

The Nelson line came to a grinding halt in the middle of nowhere. Kawatiri, in fact. The initial section, from Nelson to Foxhill, was opened in 1876, at a time when the Nelson railway was intended to be an organic, working section in its own right. It was to be a vital link in the South Island rail chain that would see Nelson, at the very top of the South Island, join up with the West Coast line, and from there on to the Greymouth – Christchurch line from the Tasman Sea to the Pacific Ocean. It was a realistic dream, and Nelson already had a rail heritage.

After all, the Dun Mountain Mining Company constructed and operated New Zealand's first railway in Nelson. Despite challenging country, the Dun Mountain Railway led the way, with a 21 km link from its chromite mine to the port of Nelson. In 1862 Nelsonians celebrated the line's opening vociferously, in the belief that with the incursion of railways, mineral extraction and transportation would translate into prosperity for the otherwise isolated province. Further inland greater mineral wealth was waiting to be tapped, and the notion of a line to Foxhill was greeted with much excitement. However, financial and trading constraints spoiled the party atmosphere and as the years passed the Dun Mountain railway lost financial viability. Mining ceased, the Dun Mountain Company shut up shop, and in 1866 the line withered and died. Despite its demise, plans were afoot to construct a far more ambitious and far-reaching railway.

As early as 1867 a survey of the proposed route had been undertaken by Henry Wrigg, who traversed over 350 km, all the way from Nelson to Cobden, on the northern banks of the Grey. Greymouth lay just across the river. Further evidence that the Nelson link was regarded as a serious undertaking came in 1871, with its inclusion on a list of proposed national trunk lines.

In 1873, a Nelson construction firm, Scott and Robertson, began work on the Nelson – Foxhill link. At the same time locomotives, carriages, brake vans and goods wagons were ordered. The Nelson to Foxhill section was the Nelson railway for several years. In its first year of operation nearly 50,000 passenger journeys were recorded and locals from Bishopdale, Stoke, Richmond, Appleby, Hope, Brightwater, Spring Grove, Wakefield,

Previous page
A train skirting the Nelson waterfront where the Nelson Express used to run.
ATL-026715-G

Leading the way, the Dun Mountain Railway, New Zealand's first, is seen here in 1862.

ATL-160121-F

Wai-iti and Foxhill flocked to the new railway. For fifty years the Nelson line's construction continued to eat into the hinterland. The railway became an accepted and acceptable adjunct to life in Nelson province, and in 1926 railway history was made.

Monday, 6 December 1926 was a red-letter day. Christmas was approaching and citizens of Nelson and its hinterland were in seasonal high spirits. 'To Greymouth in a day' had become a rail-based mantra, the notion of travelling all the way from Nelson city to Greymouth on the West Coast, utilising existing railway lines and intermediate coach services. And this was to be the wonderful day when just such a service was to be instigated.

The Nelson Express, consisting of two carriages hauled by a WF steam engine, pulled out of Nelson station at 7.40 in the morning with the intention of linking with service cars at Glenhope. The latter was designated as the railhead for the express, although earlier the same year the 7 km extension to Kawatiri had been opened.

The dream of one day being able to travel all the way to the West Coast by rail was one step closer. And of course, with Greymouth now linked with Christchurch thanks to the completion of the Otira Tunnel on the Midland Line, the heady notion of a continuous Nelson to Christchurch train journey took on a renewed aura. Mind you, there were only four passengers on the new service as it pulled out of Nelson, although more travellers joined the train at country stations along the route to Glenhope.

Locals blamed the lack of advertising for the moderate initial patronage. The fact that the new express was also designed to carry through-passengers off the inter-island ferry — either the *Arahura* or *Ngaio* — ironically drove numbers down. The ferries didn't operate on Sunday nights, so there could be no influx from that source on the Monday morning.

Locals who did avail themselves of the new service were chipper enough. Not only were they able to stretch out and enjoy the ride without jostling for seats, they could contemplate the promise of exciting times on the West Coast in relative style. The express carriages were far more comfortable than some of the older cars used on the usual mixed goods trains, which could be a bit of a mixed blessing, involving much shunting of goods wagons at rural stations with passengers having to bide their time. As a consequence timetables were unpredictable and late running common. As the engine steamed efficiently beyond Bishopdale the driver, George Bowen, and his fireman, Douglas Nickless, seemed to be rising to the excitement and sense of occasion. Thomas Russell, the guard, whose compartment occupied the rear section of the second carriage, had a spring in his stride.[1]

The train had no trouble mounting the steep grade up to Bishopdale, the first station beyond the main city terminal. Not at all like the time schoolboys coated the rails with dripping, causing a heavily laden train to slip and shudder.

The passengers talked about the novelty of connecting with service cars at Glenhope, which would take the lucky ones all the way to Reefton. Here another express was waiting to whisk them southwards towards the Grey River Valley and Greymouth, where the river met the Tasman. It made for a long day's journey — the best part of twelve hours — but would unveil dramatic bush-clad scenery in the lee of steep mountains, and burbling streams and roaring rivers, particularly the mighty Grey.

'To Greymouth in a day' relied on connections keeping to tight schedules and the Nelson Express played its part. It reached Glenhope at exactly 10.37am, it's programmed arrival time, which seemed an auspicious beginning to an historic link.

The passengers, including those who joined the train at the settlements of Richmond, Hope, Brightwater, Spring Grove, Wakefield and Foxhill, also chattered about the return service from Greymouth, which would transfer travellers to road transport at Reefton and link up with the return Nelson Express, scheduled to leave for Nelson from Glenhope at 4pm. All being well the express would reach Nelson port, beyond the main city station, at 6.49pm, in good time to connect with the ferry for the night crossing to Wellington.

The precise times of arrival — 10.37 and 6.49 — caused much light-hearted banter. Locals were too used to the wayward timetables of the mixed trains to not either cock a snook at the difficulties of adhering to such deadlines, or marvel at the determination of rail officials to at least make the attempt.

As the express climbed inland some passengers were able to recall earlier days of excitement on the Nelson line, and when the express steamed across Eden Road, just north of Brightwater, someone recounted an accident on the line, which at first looked as if the very worst had befallen several occupants of a van struck on the crossing. The vehicle involved was the Brightwater butcher's van which, as it was spun around by the force of the collision, lost its load, with chunks of meat covering a significant area, and strings of sausages hanging from fence posts and tree branches. There were no human casualties, although the van driver was shaken and several meat orders remained unfilled.

As the train reached Wakefield a passenger recalled the time a train was delayed by a stationmaster who was also a keen cricketer. The signal was set on stop at Wakefield station while the stationmaster was batting doggedly at the nearby domain. He may have been a cricketer but he was not necessarily a good one. Nine times out of ten he was dismissed long before any disruption to regular services occurred. However, cricket's a funny game, and on this particular Saturday the stationmaster played the innings of his life.

He was on his way to a century when he became aware of a train whistle sounding continuously and increasingly indignantly, for there appeared to be no obstruction on the line or at Wakefield Station. With his own show of indignation the stationmaster flailed one last ball to the boundary before allowing the next delivery to shatter his stumps. He ran to his bike, discarding pads, bat and box along the way, pedalled furiously to the station, and dropped the signal.

Despite political prevarication leading to delays in decision-making and construction, and disillusionment amongst the people of Nelson, many of them still believed the line had a future as a viable link with the West Coast. Wasn't today's jaunt on this first Nelson Express a tangible development?

Beyond Wakefield the line began to climb. Beyond Belgrove the 1 in 40 grade to the summit of the Spooner Tunnel was taken in stride, the engine working earnestly. The down-grade towards Kohatu began in the tunnel and when daylight was breached the express was gathering speed dramatically. More steady climbing was necessary on the way up to Tadmor, and further south a herculean effort pulled the train over the 445-metre saddle. From that point there was a discernible drop down towards Glenhope.

Two male passengers, one an older gent, the other a young swash-buckler, mounted a strenuous discussion as the train mounted the grade towards the Spooner Tunnel. With the benefit of hindsight the older man was able to dampen youthful ardour by recalling that by 1894 the Midland Railway Company, charged with advancing the line, had managed to cover only 11 km south of Belgrove. The government of the day was so incensed, claiming a breach of contract by the troubled Midland Railway Company, it stepped in, rolled up its figurative sleeves, and attempted to hasten proceedings.

'Be fair, old timer,' the young man said. 'I wasn't even in nappies when such shenanigans unfolded. Indeed I was still a twinkle in my father's eye.'

The old man grunted. He continued his somewhat negative stance by citing the other new South Island express service instituted on the same day as the Nelson Express, now bucking along beside the Motueka River. The other train, far beyond the local hills and mountains, was heading for Parnassus in North Canterbury, at that time the railhead of the main north line. The authorities had taken the time to liven up its carriages by painting them rich Midland Red, in a new endeavour to present more attractive trains and get away from the prevailing drab Pullman Green.

'Garish red,' the young man retorted. 'I would, sir, far rather travel in formal green through our green countryside. Red is somewhat ostentatious and perhaps a disincentive to take the train.'

The fact that the new Christchurch – Parnassus train also boasted steam-heated carriages with electric lights and swank, upholstered seating for passengers' comfort, were additional features with which the old man was able to score points against his rather garrulous and untutored young travelling companion.

Passengers who caught the Nelson Express at Tadmor walked in on the lively debate. Unperturbed by the exchange, they saw the verbal haranguing, good-natured in many ways, as the time-honoured locking of horns between the generations. The Tadmor contingent were prepared to accept the new service for what it could lead to, rather than what it lacked in sophisticated developments. And anyway, by 1927 the service also boasted Midland Red, when the train for the Duke of York's Nelson run was rolled out.

At Matupiko, encountered not long after the express had cleared the Spooner Tunnel, a partying railway worker from Kiwi, further to the south, had once run out of beer and sought replenishment at Grindles of Matupiko. A railway jigger was available on the line and was quickly seconded for the mercy dash.

After arriving back at Kiwi the hijacker left the jigger on the line, forgetting it was Thursday and a late train was due. The train driver increased speed when he saw the obstacle and was able to catapult the jigger off the

The royal train for the Duke of York nearing Dunedin in 1927. The Nelson Railway had its own royal train in the same year – and Midland Red carriages.
ATL-APG-0979-1/2-G

line. Most of the detonators carried as warning devices on jiggers went off, and the sleeping guard was jolted from his slumber, no doubt assuming, not unreasonably, that the Germans had invaded.

As the train continued its excellent timekeeping through Kiwi and along the Tadmor River Plains, positivity returned as passengers recalled earlier highlights on the line. Why, even as far back as 1909, during the lucrative years beyond 1906, Thomas Edwards, the Nelson stationmaster-in-charge, had proffered the idea of an express service when Saturday evening shopping in Nelson city was re-introduced. It would run to and from Tadmor in summer, connect with coaches and mails at Kohatu and arrive back in Nelson in time for a night out on the town.

And what about the 1908 'People's Day at the A & P Show Special', which carried 1000 passengers. It took three engines to propel the long train. Admittedly those were the heady days when Nelsonians utilised the railway to the fullest although, even in 1932, the Friday train, commonly referred to as the 'Woolworth's Special' would bring back fond memories and one or two bargains.

When a school-age girl joined the train, recollections surfaced regarding the school trains, which carried pupils to learning establishments in the city. Without the rail many young minds would not have flourished, such was the perceived importance of formal education. Logically and logistically the trains could only serve the Nelson schools from as far inland as Belgrove.

As early as 1880 thirty boys utilised the trains and three years later, when the girls' college was established, both sexes were carried. Fanny Malcolm was credited with being the first enrolled pupil of Nelson Girls. Passengers recalled how Fanny had been pushed to the front of a clutch of nervous first-day pupils because she was the oldest — and tallest. It was worth noting that Fanny had arrived by train from Richmond. She was a 'train girl'.[2]

Initially rules were lax on the school trains but, as nature dictated, boys tended to make nuisances of themselves. Soon segregated carriages were introduced. Another man who boarded the 1926 express at Brightwater, remembered the time back in 1888 when boys were turfed out of the girls' carriage. He had been one of the boys. 'They said we were behaving badly and using questionable language, but really we were just being boys.'

Such was the efficacy of train travel for school pupils that by the 1930s an unusual composition of early morning and late afternoon trains emerged. One carriage was allocated to the boys from Nelson College, another to the girls from Nelson Girls College, and a third to pupils from the convent and technical school — and the general public. In the Nelson tradition of mixed trains being the common modus operandi, several freight wagons were incorporated. Strict guidelines had been laid down and prefects were appointed to ensure that the boys did not enter the girls' carriage — and vice versa.

Despite that it was little wonder that pupils regarded the train ride as a sanctuary of sorts, a basically unsupervised environment where all hell could break loose. The boys used to rock the flimsy carriages, with their poor suspension and lateral seating, screw down the carriage brake on curves and in other ways impede progress. On one occasion, in the interests of arriving late for school, someone released the carriage brake, with the result that the train swept through Victoria Square, the closest stop serving the college, and was not brought to a halt until it was near Auckland Point School, on the extension to Nelson Port.

Reefton or bust. Intrepid passengers took the Newman's service car, like this Cadillac 353 V8, once the train reached Glenhope.

ATL-003864-G

While all this jollity and recollection unravelled, the Nelson Express beyond Kiwi passed two further settlements with bird names — Tui and Kaka. The land had become rugged and many steep-sided streams were crossed as the line climbed to the top of the Tadmor Saddle. Beyond the summit the line descended to the junction with the Little Hope River. Thoughts had been expressed that the name Little Hope was appropriate. Even as the express steamed towards Glenhope one or two more cynical — or worldly — passengers still harboured reservations about the will of politicians to see a link with Murchison and beyond.

The Hope River itself accompanied the line as it finally approached Glenhope, and, most appropriately, hopes were raised as the inaugural Nelson Express arrived at Glenhope Station.

At Glenhope, some alighting passengers prepared to catch a return service. Further to the south a spindly road disappeared into the bush above the Hope River. Hope seemed to be all around. But some Nelsonians were old and cynical enough to believe further progress was only possible when they saw it. Yes, the track had gone further on to Kawatiri and sterling efforts would soon be made to progress the link with Murchison, but the trail of disappointment and disaffected Nelsonians regarding the line's future rankled. The longer the delays and political procrastination, the more the advent of roads and motorised transport proliferated, the less likely it became that the rugged hinterland between here and Inangahua and Reefton would ever be traversed by rail.

At the Glenhope tearooms, where most took an early lunch, the mood was optimistic. 'To Greymouth in a day' was a mantra sufficient to sharpen appetites and prompt patrons to opt for a second cup of tea. For Nelsonians that was an admittedly admirable challenge, perhaps realisable now that the Nelson Express had arrived bang on time. But the notion of getting from Nelson in the north to Greymouth on the West Coast rather begged the question of how a non-progressive Nelson rail system would deal with progress — the proliferation of roads and road transport — in a time of perennial budget constraints and lethargic public action and opinion.

By 1929 continuation of construction saw the line reach as far south as Gowan Bridge on the Buller River. Reaching the Buller River was a psychological breakthrough. Besides, 1928 had seen a general election, sweeping Sir Joseph Ward and the fledgling United Party into office. They had a mandate to advance progress on unfinished railways and in a flurry of construction all the station buildings at Gowan Bridge were erected. New construction camps appeared in the wilderness between Gowan Bridge and Longford and further south again surveyors were advancing on Inangahua down the Buller River. At the end of 1930 preparation for the line to Murchison was all but finished. All the back-breaking construction work carried out by hundreds of workers, including Lofty Blomfield, who became an international figure in the sport of wrestling, seemed justified after all.

Then the politicians stepped in and suspended all work on the line, citing the Great Depression as a major deterrent. All the inherent promise in the 1926 running of the Nelson Express had came to nothing.

The Nelson line died. Its history as a withered link, going nowhere, is unique in New Zealand rail folklore. Many Nelsonians still dreamed of a link with the West Coast. As the impasse at the pass rammed home the message that the line was destined to wither in the hinterland of Murchison,

You don't know what you've got till it's nearly gone. Spirited protest action in Nelson in 1954 could not stop the march of motor transport. A year later the local line closed.

ATL-PAColl-7796-88

memories returned to the heady days when the Nelson railway was an important component of a unique province. A time that now belongs to a unique past, when the Nelson train took you to A & P shows and the Richmond races; to school and back; to late night shopping and booze-ups in the city; to the port and cross-strait ferries and other maritime adventures; to pick raspberry and hops. Even the Prince of Wales and other members of the British royal family, and sundry celebrities took the train from Nelson to Glenhope in the good old days. As late as 1951 John Stichbury, a well known New Zealand railways writer and critic, travelled along the course of the Nelson Express and deemed it to be a 'most interesting trip'.[3]

It was little wonder when the real threat of closure came in the 1950s that locals would express opposition. Ruth Page and her fine band of women vigilantes, including Sonja Davies, acted and spoke for the district. Their protest on the tracks was one of the first signs that a women's revolution was barely a decade away. When I was a boy we had all heard about the brave women who, in 1955, sat on the Nelson lines in an attempt to force the male rail establishment to reconsider the closure of their railway. Ruth

Page, Sonja Davies and seven cohorts stopped the demolition train at the lonely, symbolically named Kiwi siding.

Meanwhile the embankments and preparation for rail progress beyond Glenhope and Kawatiri faded into the foliage. Today the ghost railway groundwork is still visible, with the formations for tracks that were never laid continuing almost to Murchison.

Of all the provincial rail systems in New Zealand, the Nelson network holds a special fascination. From its inception to its controversial closure in 1955, it was always a stand-alone operation.

No reprieve. Prime Minister Keith Holyoake is represented in a 1957 cartoon, refusing to fund extensions to the Nelson tracks.

ATL-A-310-196

Twenty-one years later, in 1976, we travelled by car through a territory once reverberating with the sound of a live, steam-driven railway. In a lonely paddock somewhere near the old rail-bed of the Nelson railway, a level-crossing sign emblazoned with the name Spring Grove caught the eye. We stopped and took a photo. Time marched on.

Time had further to march in 1953 when Lawrence Constable, in *Home Territory*, wrote about the strangulation of the Nelson line.

> But as the hills close in and the long climb begins to the heights of Hope Saddle, the forest reaches over from Westland. Above the wooded hills of the foreground, range upon range, the high points of three provinces lift into view; then the road falls swiftly to Glenhope in the upper basin of the Buller. The railway ends here, twenty miles short of Murchison. But beyond Glenhope a ghost train runs through cuttings, tunnels, stations, embankments — all of them empty of rails. Many years have passed since work ceased on the Glenhope — Inangahua section. The country is formidable, but if we are to believe Nelson's hampered business people, not impossible; and there is still a campaign to 'close the gap' between railheads . . .[4]

10 Don't take this train for granted

The West Coast Express, 1936

Rita Angus's painting of Cass, a tiny whistle stop on the route of the West Coast Express, is highly evocative of the unique physical setting of the Midland Line, along which the express used to run. Angus's painting dates from 1936 when the coast-to-coast train was in its prime, and the work, often regarded as our best-known railway landscape painting, was almost as famous as the West Coast Express itself.

We missed the West Coast Express by about ten years. It stopped running in 1956, to be replaced by railcars. By the time we embarked on our first rail pilgrimage through the South Island, it was 1967, and the old express was a dim memory, although you could swear that the plumes of smoke from its engine were still hanging in the sky above the Southern Alps.

Long before entrepreneurs with dollar signs in their eyes looked upon the route of the old Midland Line between Rolleston and Greymouth, local South Islanders sensed the value of the link. Magnificent mountain scenery, braided river valleys and the lush greens of the West Coast were long regarded as features of an outstanding train ride, though few realised just how popular the ride would become. As a result, the success of the TranzAlpine train, particularly with New Zealanders a long way from home and international tourists, took many locals by surprise. One man's backyard, another man's paradise, was one of many attempts to explain the majesty of the ride and why Kiwis took so long to take it on board.

Then of course, in typical Kiwi fashion, there were those who took the express and its route for granted. The Midland line was not, to them, a main line, and a trip from Christchurch to the West Coast was visiting the wrong side of the tracks. Greymouth and the other towns on the Coast were regarded as a bit grubby and working class. And then there was the rain. Sometimes it was too much about the destination and less about the physical grandeur of the journey. For a start the Southern Alps, through which the line snaked, could boast 185 peaks that rose to 2133 m or more, with 16 taller mountains topping 3050 metres.

A critical year in the emergence of the West Coast Express came in 1923, when the Otira Tunnel was finally breached and a coast-to-coast

Opposite

The West Coast Express, hauled by AB 808, rounds a bend near Greymouth.

ATL-058152-F

rail journey became possible. In 1924 the first West Coast Express made it through, and for the first time in its history, the New Zealand rail network could boast a complete coast to coast express service, from Christchurch on the Pacific Ocean in the east to Greymouth on the Tasman Sea at its western extent. Purists could point to the Onehunga suburban services that linked the east with the west in Auckland — from the Waitemata Harbour to the Manukau — but that was no express train. And the old boat trains that travelled along the same tracks, while being part of an express service, did not represent the total journey.

More than that, the West Coast Express, thanks to the Otira Tunnel was guaranteed longevity. There were no road tunnels through the mountains and air services linking the east and west coasts would not be established until the late 1960s. As a result the express remained the primary link for over 30 years.

At around 10am, one cold morning in 1936, the West Coast Express departed Christchurch station. Many passengers were coasters returning home after visiting the big smoke 'over the hill'. Others were first-time travellers who had little inkling as to what lay ahead. Some still took the train for granted. They'd done the journey many times before and had come to regard the world-class scenery as almost passé.

The initial movements were mandatory as the train headed out on the main south line, until at Rolleston, the junction with the Midland line — the 'home' of the West Coast Express — the train headed for the hills. Off in the distance the snow-covered Southern Alps beckoned as the line travelled in a series of long, straight lines across the plains, through Kirwee, Darfield and Sheffield. Earlier in the day a linking train ran from Ashburton to Darfield Junction to meet the express, before it went on to Springfield in the lee of the Torlesse Range.

The line curved north, the plains receded and the Waimakariri River swung into view. It was around midday. The contrast between the

From sea level to snow in an hour or two. A 'Snow Sports Special', c.1939, arrives at Arthur's Pass with a trainload of city slickers.

ATL-MNZ-1298-1/4-F

Canterbury Plains and the Waimakariri River and Gorge was marked. Wide braided river beds, towering mountains and narrow gorges represented the workings of natural forces, but the efforts of man were also riveting. Viaducts constructed high above rivers and streams and the many tunnels bored through rock faces were engineering feats of incredible ingenuity, daring and courage.

One of the most lauded aspects of the route was the way the train transported the traveller through scenery both diverse and diverting. Even those who took the train for granted were amazed at how, in less than seven hours, it passed through concentrated scenic delights that in other parts of the world might take two or three days. First-time travellers were totally captivated and rather surprised such a gem of rail travel had not been praised to the heavens.

The names of settlements were developing a character of their own. Kowhai Bush, Craigieburn and now Cass, subject of Rita Angus's landmark landscape painting. The line swapped the Waimakariri Gorge for that of the Bealey River as it headed northwest towards Arthur's Pass. Popular excursion trains, known as snow specials, used to carry city slickers from Christchurch to the ski fields and snow-covered regions around Arthur's Pass. In 1926 over 800 passengers travelled as far as Otira, beyond Arthur's Pass, in two special trains. On the same day another 600 took a following train to Arthur's Pass. Even in the 1950s such trains were well patronised, and by far the best way to access the wintry wastes. It wasn't uncommon to see four specials running every Sunday in the 1950s, each one carrying close to 1000 passengers.

The mountains were alive with Cantabrians, and the services incurred the wrath of the clergy because they ran on Sundays. More troubling was the fact that some patrons were less gracious than others. 'Bodgies' and 'Widgies', a troubling teenage subset of the 1950s, once ran riot at Arthur's Pass. Not only did they take the train for granted, they took anything that wasn't nailed down.

'Mystery Tramping Excursions' also became popular, as a result of the thirties' craze for tramping. Only the district the train would be going through was revealed to the passengers, with perhaps a map of the district to accompany the leaflet handed out as the mystery train left Christchurch. The leaflet also included the lyrics of sing-along songs and before long a harmonica band moved through the carriages to accompany the singers. A sense of expectation and communality developed and when the engine

Withholding a secret, normally dour railways staff betray their sense of fun. A mystery train engine, complete with noticeboard, prepares to join its train to – who knows where?

J.A.T. Terry Collection

added its own song — two long blasts on its whistle — it was time to quit the train and commence tramping.

The initial mystery train in 1932 attracted over 200 trampers and hikers, with the number climbing to 700 within five years. The route of the West Coast Express was a common conduit to uncluttered areas like the Big Kowhai River hinterland and the Staircase Gully district. Humorous encounters with life in the country lightened the city spirit. Like the English tourist who wondered aloud whether the sheep running loose in the foothills ever got lost. And the time a young city-bred lady enquired of a shepherd if the lamb lying across his saddle was wild or tame. Such larks.

What larks ahead. Thousands of Cantabrians took to the snow, many inspired by Railways publicity posters like this one.

ATL-Eph-A-RAIL-1950-01

'Mystery Tramping Excursions' were well organised and sanctioned by the Railways Department, although a less formal arrangement prevailed with a night express goods train known as The Perishable. Introduced in the mid-1920s, the train attracted hardy, more dedicated mountaineers and adventurers, who travelled in the guard's van up the Midland Line to points in the Arthur's Pass area to tilt at peaks, after enduring a typically rough ride. Travellers had to sign a document absolving the railways of any responsibility if there was an accident. Women were welcome, but only if they were accompanied by a male.

In later years The Perishable, so named not because of accidents befalling passengers, but because the train carried perishable goods from Christchurch to the coast and vice versa, was allocated a passenger carriage. This was carried directly behind the engine to enable travellers to avail themselves of the benefit of steam heating. The charm of bunking down in often unheated guard's vans — part of the train's initial rugged appeal — diminished, even more so when overnight rail cars began plying the course and weekend 'mountain dwellers' could access the great divide in greater comfort.

In 1936 the West Coast Express has reached Arthur's Pass, where the great divide is closing in. The AB engine is unhitched and English electric engines (class EO), are aligned to carry the train through the Otira Tunnel.

The electrified section is the first such feature on the New Zealand network. With the overhead wires disappearing into a bright, white distance, the European cut to the electric engines, and mountains converging from a great height, Arthur's Pass is truly New Zealand's alpine railway. It's a poor man's means of seeing Switzerland, albeit for little more than a few kilometres.

Arthur's Pass, at 737 m above sea level, is the highest station on the line. Less than four hours ago the train was at the coast in Christchurch, and already the compression of dramatically different physical environments into a seven-hour train ride is evident. Another realisation assails the senses as the express enters the Otira Tunnel. In 1936 it is the longest rail tunnel in the southern hemisphere, at 8.5 km.

Through the mountains the line dips perceptibly; with an average gradient of 1 in 33 it is quite a plunge and considered too daunting for the steam engines pulling heavy trains up the grade from the western approaches. Electric traction was the only means of preventing engine crews and express passengers becoming distressed by smoke inhalation.

The TranzAlpine waits at Arthur's Pass, the Midland Line's highest station, in more recent times.

Graham Hutchins

Other options considered as a means of linking the Canterbury rails with the West Coast included a Fell incline system, not unlike that constructed over the North Island's Rimutaka Ranges. Zigzag switchbacks and spiralling tunnels were also on the drawing board for a time, but as the express continues — and continues — to swish down through the tunnel the efficiency of the basic A to B rail tunnel is appreciated. It's easy to believe further claims that the tunnel is the longest in the British Commonwealth and one of the longest in the world, as the train shows little sign of emerging into daylight. Regular travellers take it in their stride but first-timers could be forgiven for thinking night has suddenly fallen, or a total eclipse of the sun, unscheduled by official stargazers, has suddenly occurred.

Arthur's Pass station in 1997. The alpine setting is unique, the station buildings new, but the mountains are as old as time.

Graham Hutchins

Officialdom was well represented on 4 August 1923, when the Otira Tunnel was opened. William Massey, the Prime Minister, and Gordon Coates, Minister of Public Works headed the guest list at the opening ceremony.

At Otira, while a West Coast AB is attached in lieu of the electrics, passengers have a half-hour break while dinner is served. From the tunnel the express has emerged into a new world. Westland, where the rain falls plentifully and often. Greenery glistens with recent rain; watercourses rush through native bush enclosures; lakes, or simply sheets of surface water, lie around every bend; rivers surge and run-off creates temporary waterfalls. If you'd fallen asleep in the tunnel you would have awoken to a new wonderland. If you were of a nervous disposition you might have imagined you were on the wrong train.

Beyond Aickens the line curves to accommodate the Taramakau River, which meets the sea near Kumara. The scenic contrast with eastern approaches, with their dry yellows and browns, as depicted by Rita Angus, is all but total. Bush, flax, forest and the occasional open areas run through the gamut of green tones. Cabbage trees and nikau palms stand reflected in clear, pure pools or disappear as sudden downpours disturb the surface. Even hillocks and the foothills themselves are cloaked in dense vegetation. If other reaches of New Zealand where bush has been cleared can be described as resembling human stubble, with hills rising on both sides of the track like a man’s face short of the razor, then Westland’s hills sport full beards.

After crossing the Taramakau River near Jacksons the line curves dramatically at Inchbonnie, and as the express passes Lake Poerua it is heading back virtually to the east. By the time Te Kinga, Ruru and Moana are reached the line is again holding its westward drift. Moana on Lake Brunner boasts one of the most charming station settings in New Zealand, where snow-capped peaks are reflected in the still, green waters of Westland’s largest lake. The express is now 198 km from Christchurch and little more than 37 km from Greymouth.

The Arnold River, flowing out of Lake Brunner, accompanies the line through Kotuku, Kaimata and Kokiri to Stillwater, where the Arnold meets the Grey and the incomplete Westport line connects with the Midland. In 1936 construction recommenced on the Stillwater – Westport connection. The Great Depression led to the curtailment of work in 1931, but now, some months after the Labour Government won the 1935 election, hundreds of construction workers are deployed to hasten the line’s completion. Seven years later the link would be working.

The line from Stillwater to Reefton was completed in 1907, and passengers from the express change at Stillwater for Ngahere, Ahaura, Ikamatua and Reefton. Meanwhile the final half hour of the journey sees the line hug the banks of the Grey. If the workings of nature had dominated much of the journey, the final kilometres reveal the hand of man.

The old Brunner industrial site on the Grey used to unearth twice as much coal as any other New Zealand coal mine. Thousands of firebricks were made here too, until in 1896 a mining disaster claimed the lives of 67, leading to the downgrading of the whole complex, although in 1936 it’s still operational. Beyond Dobson, another mining settlement, the train eased into Greymouth station.

It's fair to say that the West Coast Express meant more to West Coasters than it did to those living in Christchurch and areas further to the east. Most coasters just called it 'the express'. The West Coast had always had an isolated, outpost aspect, a region hidden beyond the mountains that seemed more resistant to change than others. Travellers, on first encountering the 'Coast', remarked how much like an earlier version of New Zealand towns like Greymouth, Westport and Hokitika appeared. Locals, in their turn, were proud of their traditions and maverick tendencies in a rugged hinterland bordered by the broken, driftwood-strewn beaches of the Tasman and rain-drenched foothills to the east. Physical, often dangerous, industries like coal mining, forestry and fishing sustained the region. They were thirst-generating occupations and the coast became infamous for the number of pubs it boasted per head of population, as well as for the odd hours those pubs observed at a time when the harsh strictures of six o'clock closing swept the nation.

The West Coast Express became an institution. Despite local loyalties to the region and its often harsh environment — incessant rainfall, challenging working conditions and somewhat smoke and coal-stained communities — the express represented a means of escape to the wider world 'over the hill'.

Escaping was occasionally a challenge in itself. In 1940 serious flooding disrupted the passage of the express both to and from the West Coast, a not uncommon occurrence. In the *New Zealand Railways Magazine* Rev W. A. Curzon-Siggers of St Martin's Vicarage, North East Valley, Dunedin, was especially commendatory in praising the Greymouth stationmaster for making alternative transport arrangements, necessitated by the 1940 floods.[1]

Even on a good day, while travelling south from Greymouth to Hokitika on the express feeder service (often referred to as the Hokitika Passenger southbound), a certain distinctive rusticity remains evident.

Writer Lawrence Constable described his first impressions of Hokitika in the following manner, after travelling by train down the coast from Greymouth:

> The approach to Hokitika is not one of the charms for which the Coast is famous. Arriving by rail, one is suddenly surrounded by houses in want of paint. A stern feudal-looking church watches over them, forbidding any more levity of the gold-rush kind. Above all, one is conscious of what might be called the theme of Hokitika: corrugated iron. 'Hokey' owns more of it, much more, than its quota. There are acres of it, imparting the proper air of an outpost of the empire.[2]

He may have also mentioned warped hotels, potholes and rotting wharves but he went on to laud the fact that the spirit of New Zealand's past was 'surviving so fiercely'. And the people were friendly and sociable. They waved at passing trains, the way all New Zealanders used to.

In 1967 we might have missed the express by ten years, but when we first travelled south to catch the Christchurch – Greymouth railcar it missed us. Or rather it only went as far as Springfield because a slip at Otira, after ten days of West Coast rain, had blocked the line. Ten days rain. In Canterbury, on the other side of the ranges, there had been a virtual drought during the same period. One or two showers, we were told. So all this disappointing talk of cancelled services must have been the result of an earthquake, such was our ignorance of the West Coast's unique microclimate.

And we missed the Greymouth – Westport railcar by one month. We arrived in October 1967 while the service up the Buller Gorge was withdrawn in September. We knew most other passenger services on West Coast branches had bitten the dust. Coal dust specifically. The Blackball branch and the Seddonville line north of Westport both lost their passenger services way back in the 1940s — so having to catch a sterile Road Services bus from Springfield to Greymouth, via the Lewis Pass, after de-training at Springfield, hardly put a spring in our step.

In 1971 we finally revisited the West Coast by railcar, in the middle of a rainstorm. The Grey River welcomed us to Greymouth by playfully lapping its engorged waters at the ballast alongside the track. The waters at Stillwater were anything but still — they surged. Stillwater was still the junction for the Buller line up to Westport and our railcar struggled into sheets of water falling from a dark grey sky. Everything was grey. The Grey River, Greymouth, even the beer served in seven-ounce glasses in a murky, grey pub across from the station. Fellow drinkers, coal miners mainly, sported grey faces where the rain had diluted coal dust from around their eyes — which may have been grey too if we could have seen them. Light bulbs swayed and flickered as the thunder roared, or was that the sound of the Tasman dashing its grey-white water on the grey sand beach?

But we loved the place. The warmth of the locals, once they'd got to know you; the comfort of the old hotel's bedroom, despite condensation oozing down the puckered scrim walls. The whitebait fritters, flounder-like turbot and warm beer all had their own way of adding colour to the West Coast canvas. Then there was the train ride from Greymouth up the Rewanui Incline. Across the swollen river, where debris clung to the bridge struts as if reluctant to confront the confluence with the ocean, the grubby train grunted through Runanga and Dunollie and on to the incline. It remains one of the most remarkable train rides of our frequent pilgrimages. We may have been too late for other services but we nailed the Rewanui Incline.

Back in 1971 you had to strike while the iron was hot. Rail services were likely to be closed virtually behind you, as the hot iron cooled.

It had been a long journey from Christchurch to Greymouth. The railcar in 1971 carried on as far south as Hokitika and the railhead at Ross. Night was falling as we pulled into Hokitika. It had been a triumphal trip, finally making the West Coast along the route of the West Coast Express, after being thwarted in 1967 by the slip. In a light-headed moment we decided to call it quits, despite knowing there were another 20 or so kilometres of virgin track to Ross, beyond Hokitika. We had become so enamoured of the Coast we could see no reason why we shouldn't return in the near future, when we would go to the end of the line.

A few months later the extension between Hokitika and Ross was closed to railcar traffic, probably for the very reason we had alighted at Hokitika. Other casual travellers, equally smitten by the rugged charms of the Coast probably also had it in mind to return. In the meantime, worn down by weariness and the onset of night, they opted for Hokitika, thinking like us, that tomorrow's another day. But this time it wasn't.

Patronage to Ross was already declining. We should have grasped the nettle and gone to the end of the West Coast line when we could. Yet one of the last trains to paradise survives in the form of the world-renowned TranzAlpine train from Christchurch to Greymouth. It doesn't go all the way to Ross, or Hokitika, but it goes far enough to showcase the old route of the West Coast Express to the world. And obviously, like the old express, it doesn't take long to express itself.

Russell Young wrote in 1997 after travelling on the TranzAlpine:

> It is not long before the magic commences. The upper reaches of the Waimakariri are probed and we climb through Craigieburn, Cass and Cora Lynn. The open-air viewing car is a boon for windswept photographers. Crashing views down to the rushing upper reaches are split by noisy entrance into tunnels and eerie emergence on to the giddying viaducts. It just seems too easy to split the Southern Alps, yet here there are broad brown plains heading to yet another crease through the hills, until finally we reach Arthur's Pass. We are reminded just how far we have climbed when parts of the platform are inches thick in solid ice, the sun not reaching this valley floor. Then we are rushing through the mighty Otira Tunnel to emerge in the green-grey landscapes of Westland. The magic continues when Lake Brunner hoves into view out the left window, with a picture postcard snow-capped mountain backdrop. Two cans of Steinlager later, we pull into Greymouth.

11 To the rugby on the 'Rocky Island Line'

The Test Match Special, 1956

Rugby, as well as the railways, helped define New Zealand. 'Rugby specials', whether they were taking fans to test-match city or Ranfurly Shield challenges, were a constant presence on the New Zealand rail network at a time when excursion trains were almost as common as the expresses and limiteds.

The popularity of the Ranfurly Shield — and the trains that carried supporters — was profound. A shield match in Christchurch in the early 1930s attracted three special trains from Invercargill, which equated to 1500 passengers. Four trains from the West Coast ferried 2000 more.

In the very early days special trains took fans to rugby matches, before the Ranfurly Shield had even been established as the apex of inter-provincial supremacy, and before test match rugby became a regular winter celebration. In 1893 New Zealand Railways, Wellington Section, announced details of a special train set to travel from the central city to Petone, where 'football matches' were scheduled to be played.

> On Saturday, 13th instant, a Special Train, not stopping at Kaiwarra [Kaiwharawhara] nor Ngahauranga [Ngauranga], will leave Te Aro at 2.30pm and Wellington at 2.38pm. Return train will leave Petone at 5.18pm. Return tickets, including admission to ground-carriages, 1s 6d; seated trucks, 1s.[1]

Further on during the golden age, when the railways was such a bounteous employer and rugby prevailed as the working man's religion, it was not surprising that the department established its own representative rugby team. They even had their own symbol of supremacy — the Football Challenge Cup. In 1927 teams representing the locomotive staff of Canterbury and Otago provinces slugged it out in lousy weather for the right to hold the cup aloft.

W. H. H. Grapes, reporting in the *New Zealand Railways Magazine*, revealed the success of the Otago team and went on to postulate on the significance of such matches in terms of unity within the railways environment.

Previous page

An AB-headed excursion train at Hamilton station in 1949. Test match specials often looked like this – nothing special.

J.A.T. Terry Photo

> Following the usual custom a reception was given to the visiting team in the evening. Speeches appropriate to the occasion were delivered by Mr W. Pullar (chairman), and by Mr L. Woodford (manager of the Canterbury team), and a programme of varied items was enjoyed by all present. The enthusiasm and good fellowship which characterises these annual matches (and the subsequent receptions) has a lasting influence for good on the morale of the service.[2]

The railways, as well as rugby, continued to help define New Zealand. Many prominent rugby players and administrators worked for the railways during the years when trains ruled the transport landscape. William 'Massa' Johnston, masseur for the 1934 All Blacks who beat Australia 2–1 in a test series in Australia, was also a leading referee, after playing for his country in 1905 and 1907. Just as significant was his feat of working for the railways for 30 years as a cleaner, fireman and driver. He may well have worked on a test-match special, which would have been entirely appropriate: an AB working on an AB engine.

Was it any wonder that rugby specials took on a semi-sacred significance during the golden era? The trains were glory-bound, particularly when the All Blacks developed the habit of winning most of their games.

The test-match special *was* special. Travellers looked forward to getting to the game as much as they enjoyed the game itself. The camaraderie and expectation was as much about the All Black's chances, as it was about the chances of finding friends for life on the rollicking, inevitably boozy trains headed for test-match city.

The true spirit of the test-match special was best exemplified when rugby followers were obliged to catch the train in the depths of night. Taumarunui used to be a departure point for trains heading for Auckland and Eden Park. No one knew for sure when exactly the train left, but test-match specials were never about punctuality and exact adherence to details. That was women's stuff. The Taumarunui train used to come into Te Kuiti at about four in the morning. Or five.

K 909 waits in the Taumarunui yard in 1950. The K engines were once compared to front-row forwards in rugby: big, bustling, no-nonsense. It was appropriate that they should pull the test match specials.

J.A.T. Terry Photo

Blokes had gathered at the station as early as three, never really sure when the bugger would arrive. Rugby was a winter sport, and three in the morning in towns like Te Kuiti was a challenge. Fog floated down. Failing that, the breeze chilled your bones. Unless it was raining of course, which it often was. In later years of the golden era, at least the pie cart, pulsing just beyond the station, was a sanctuary. Pie and chips for breakfast would put a lining on the stomach. Those who failed to avail themselves of such padding often consigned themselves to various states of alcoholic oblivion.

Even in urban centres test-match specials departed in the middle of the night. It wasn't just farmers and small-town merchants who found themselves clustering on frost-flecked stations as the steam-hauled special thundered out of the dark. In 1956, a pivotal year for rugby in New Zealand, writer Gordon Slatter and his mates travelled from Christchurch to Dunedin to see the first test of the epochal series between the All Blacks and the Springboks.

> The special left about midnight; Guds and I shared a double seat and Syd was across the aisle. We had hired pillows but there wasn't much sleep

> to be had that night. The train was packed; passengers had turned the seating into alcoves, passengers roamed along the carriages banging the doors open and greeting their acquaintances with guffaws. The bloke in the corner seat twanging the guitar was apparently unable to play any tune but 'The Rock Island Line'. Bottles rolled and crashed under the seats. The constable on duty ambled through with a tolerant smile. Nobody in the card school at our end of the carriage wanted the lights off; the hats on the chrome hooks nodded solemn approval.[3]

These were deeply conservative times. Egalitarianism was rampant. Tall poppies were plucked. Even the All Blacks were expected to reflect the 'average is excellent' tag. Fast wingers were suspect, as were tall half-backs and intellectual locks. Wingers were best if they were earnest plodders who pinned their ears back and went for the corner. Half-backs were expected to be short, nuggetty and heroic. And if you had a PhD in something, you couldn't hope to be whistled up into the forward pack.

Ron Jarden playing for Wellington in 1950. Sometimes he was too nifty for his own good: a fast 'tall poppy' at a time when we were all supposed to be average hewers.

ATL-114/161/11-G

On the homeward journey of the test-match special from Dunedin all anyone could talk about was Ron Jarden, the All Black winger. As the train gathered speed around the moonlit fringes of Otago Harbour, it was Ron Jarden this and Ron Jarden that. Jarden was one of those really quick sprinters who inflamed the emotions of a certain type of Kiwi. Apparently he couldn't tackle, and he wouldn't go for the corner. The thing was, in the first test at Carisbrook, Jarden had won the game and the All Blacks went one-up in the series. Jarden scored seven of the All Blacks' 10 points, including an audacious intercept try from halfway that wrapped up the game. You needed to be a suspect sprinter to have scored that try.

The guard wandered through as the debate heated up. Jarden was all right after all. He may have been a sprinter, but he could kick goals and he did make a tackle or two. But still there were those, after a bottle or two too many, as the return train went through the 'marus'— Oamaru and Timaru — who reckoned Jarden's try was pure luck.

By now the test-match special was a party on wheels. Away from the strictures of the wife and six o'clock closing, a day of days was celebrated. The guitars chunked, empty bottles continued to roll and clunk and the guard turned a blind eye. New Zealand had enjoyed a superb day. The All Blacks had beaten the champion Boks, and the railways had made much of it possible. The war was over, the golden weather of the post-war years glowed, even though the temperature outside was minus something. Inside, the toasty warmth of the steam-heated carriages drove demons away.

Everyone drank a toast to everyone else, but no one thought of drinking a toast to the train. Trains were just part of 1950s reality. Even the vanquished Springboks would be travelling up the same tracks in their specially designated Vulcan railcar. They had a match to play against combined South Canterbury, Mid-Canterbury and North Otago in Timaru, just as soon as they'd licked their wounds and drowned their sorrows after their first test loss.

The Springboks' railcar was quite a talking point, even in the mid-1950s when train travel was taken for granted. In fact two railcars — a Standard model in the North Island and a Vulcan in the South Island, had been allocated to augment their air travel. From Whangarei in the north and as far south as Dunedin the Springbok railcars became a fascinating if temporary part of the cluttered New Zealand rail environment. They travelled as far west in the North Island as New Plymouth, and as far east as Gisborne. In the South Island, as well as taking the main trunk route, they ventured west on the Midland Line as far as Westport. In all, more than 3380 km of territory was traversed by the railcars and the occasional railways bus. The tourists saw local rail wonders such as the Raurimu Spiral on the North Island main trunk, the Mohaka Viaduct, the country's tallest, during the railcar leg between Napier and Gisborne, and the longest tunnel in the Commonwealth through the Rimutakas on the journey between Wellington and Masterton. Between Timaru and Christchurch, New

Zealand's longest bridge across the 1.6 km-wide Rakaia River would have raised a few eyebrows.

As the test-match special slowed to cross the same bridge, on-board celebrations continued to rage. The mood of the passengers was even more raucous than on the journey down to Dunedin. More beer was drunk and the singing drowned out any sounds the train could make. For those feeling the worse for wear there was no escape, not like the rugby fan who stepped off a test-match special later that season as it stopped momentarily in the Whangamarino wetlands, on the way home from the deciding test match in Auckland. The queue to the toilets was altogether too challenging and he thought he'd answer the call of nature when the train made an unscheduled stop.

The stillness of the ballast-strewn ground after the lurch and sway of the carriage disorientated his booze-inflamed senses and he found himself listing and tumbling into a swampy recess. By the time he'd extracted himself the train had picked up surprising speed, a bit like Peter Jones when he scored his 'buggering' try in the day's test match — the final game of 1956 — and the shivering fan was left alone to contemplate a lonely, darkening backwater and not too many lights off in the distance.

The memory of Peter Jones' match-clincher kept his spirits up as he clumped down the tracks. That and the feeling the triumphant All Blacks were not too far removed in egalitarian New Zealand from himself and the other baying fans on the terraces. He and his mates were not too surprised to see Bill Gray, the All Black strongman in mid-field, waiting for a train at Auckland Station to take him back to the Bay of Plenty. Bill Gray, a hero in the 1956 series, was joining the exodus from test-match city just like any other ordinary joker.

Meanwhile, beyond the Rakaia Bridge, Gordon Slatter and his companion on the home-bound special from Dunedin found the day catching up with them.

> Guds and I were both feeling dragged but in contrast everybody else seemed hilarious and the 'Rock Island Line' carried more freight than

> ever. I sat staring dully at the ladies toilet sign, which had the 'i' scratched out, thinking what an unfunny lot our countrymen are, even though they can win rugby tests.[4]

The rugby specials were a male domain. The ladies were not so much scratched out, they were simply otherwise detained. Someone had to look after the kids and keep the home fires burning. Gender roles were sharply delineated back then. Men brought home the bacon, women cooked it. Men fought in wars, women grieved. Women had babies, men followed the rugby. It was just the way things were. Men followed the rugby — literally. Rugby specials served that purpose. Even the men who enabled men in general to follow the rugby — engine drivers — were swept up in the passionate following of rugby.

J. M. Grainger, in his book *On and Off the Rails,* wrote about a crew who piloted a train to a race meeting in a small country town and found themselves with time to kill before the return train was set to depart. They visited the local billiards saloon, and had a meal and a beer or two at the hotel. Meanwhile, the steam engine waiting back at the station should have had its fire maintained to enable a quick getaway once the races were over. All would have been well if the crew had returned to the train after the billiards, nosh and beer. However, the game of rugby got in the way and the crew could not resist.

> They had been told that the local football team was to engage in combat with its deadliest rivals at the domain, a few hundred yards down the road. A short sit in the sun while they smoked a cigarette and they were off to see the football. Life was good indeed.[5]

When they finally scrambled back to their engine the fire had gone out. The train was due to depart, and in desperation they seconded several railway tarpaulins for fuel. Luckily this provided an adequate, if smoky, foundation for the fire to be reignited. Luckily too, the racegoers were late getting back to the station and the train was able to leave under its own steam.

It had been a decidedly 'rugby, racing and beer' day in times when the three-pronged symbol of a male-dominated society prevailed. Not that society always approved of such a trifecta, particularly when good-natured bonhomie lapsed into mayhem. Drunken shambles on rugby excursions and sports trains in general was sometimes a problem.

As far back as 1904 a train carrying Dunedin's Alhambra and Union rugby club sides to and from Christchurch arrived home bejewelled with broken glass, discarded food, general rubbish and vomit. In 1937 a test-match train transporting Taranaki supporters to Auckland carried on the tradition. Carriage windows were broken, toilets blocked and further evidence of excessive alcohol consumption did little for the reputation of the railways and rugby followers.

All due decorum on this race day train in the early 1900s, but sometimes all hell broke loose on rugby excursions and sports trains.

ATL-PA1-Q-100-22-3

In more recent times, I travelled on a train not designated a rugby special, although it might well have been. The mid-morning mixed train, number 437, took some mates and me from Te Kuiti to Taumarunui, ostensibly to watch a Saturday match between King Country and Thames Valley. The lone carriage held about 10 passengers, all of whom were heading for the big game. A knot of older fans began uncorking quart bottles even as the train began its stuttering climb up the Waitete embankment. My mates and I were still schoolboys and at that time — the early 1960s — most schoolboys were not in the habit of drinking on trains heading for the rugby. The older fans got stuck in though, every beer accompanied by a leer in our direction. The toilet door, for no apparent reason, was wedged shut. Perhaps it was locked by railway staff who reckoned no one travelled on the mixed trains any more and those who did wouldn't need to use the ablution block at the head of the carriage.

The older fans did and it was no surprise to us when they took to urinating off the balcony of the old wooden carriage, as the long train snaked over Waitete Viaduct and through the Porootarao Tunnel, as it disappeared deeper into the heart of the King Country.

It was a good day, in the sense that King Country beat Thames Valley. I'm not too sure what happened to the schedules relating to the departure of the return train — or the kick-off time at Rugby Park, Taumarunui. Both seemed a bit skew-whiff. The train left earlier than anticipated, and the kick-off was at 3.00pm, not 2.30, as scheduled. We were forced to leave the park early, at a time when King Country were comfortably enough placed, at 13–6, not learning until later that the home side upped the ante in the final quarter to take the game 21–6, but we were happy enough.

It had been a great way to get to the rugby, and we made a sound decision to forfeit watching half an hour of a game that was in the bag. Don't know about the older fans, who had been adamant, in a beery sort of way, that they had return tickets — and would be honouring them.

Being stranded in Taumarunui did not appeal, although the older fans probably continued drinking at the after-match function and the local clubs until closing time, before being consigned to a lonely vigil on Taumarunui station until the northbound express arrived in the early hours of the morning. Even then, because they weren't booked on the express they may have had to wait even longer for the limited, which they weren't booked on either. It may have been a case of sleeping fitfully on the hard station seats until the following day's mixed train set out. They would have had any number of spare seats on that. (Several weeks later we learned the mixed train didn't run on Sundays. Perhaps the older fans are still in Taumarunui).

At least Gordon Slatter, off the test-match special between Christchurch and Dunedin in 1956, made it home to a warm bed at the scheduled time — give or take an hour or two.

> I reached my place at last and crept into bed beside the wife, who was a bit pipped with me because she had been up to the boy half the night. I felt terrible, my head was sore, my throat was sore, but as I went off I was still saying, delirious-like, we beat 'em, we beat 'em.[6]

12 The tawny mantle of tussock

The Central Otago Express, 1939

The Central Otago line was the longest branch in New Zealand. Beyond Cromwell it went nowhere, although it traversed 237 km of unique country as it threaded its way inland beyond Dunedin. By 1939, any dream of extending the line towards Hawea, with the intention of joining up with the West Coast line at Hokitika via the Haast Pass, had long since turned to dust. God knows, it had been hard enough getting the authorities interested in so much as a road. Besides there was now a war on and expansionist plans for rail had to take a back seat.

Passengers at Dunedin Station take a seat — back, front and middle — in the old wooden carriages of the Otago Central Passenger Train. Some still call it the Central Otago Express. Certainly its relevance to the lives of those living in the rocky ramparts and tablelands of Central is a significant factor, despite the fact the line took so long to be completed. Up until 1900 mixed trains, with both goods wagons and passenger carriages together in the same train, served the backblocks to various railheads. Exclusively passenger services first ran in the years between 1900 and World War I, but mixed trains returned for over 20 years before a regular daily passenger train was reinstalled in 1936, all the way to and from Cromwell.

By 1939 the train was a popular staple on the New Zealand Railways system. Not only did it get you to Middlemarch, Hyde, Ranfurly, Alexandra, Clyde, Cromwell and countless other settlements, but the 'up' train, leaving Cromwell at 9.10am, enabled outlying farmers, merchants and others to take the train to the 'seething metropolis' of Dunedin.

A few minutes before 8am the AB engine whistles its intentions and with a decided lurch and wrench of couplings, the train moves away from Sir George Troup's singularly grand Dunedin station. As the train winds its way through the southern suburbs a flustered man, the last aboard, and then at the final possible moment, is having difficulty wedging a bulging suitcase into the overhead luggage rack. Obviously he should have used the storage facility in the guard's van but there was no time for that. Eventually

Previous page
Mum and the kids alight as the Central Otago Express stops at Ranfurly in 1950 to give AB 728 a breather.
J.A.T. Terry Photo

he gives up and parks his bag in the aisle, inevitably inciting the guard to make the stern suggestion that the bulging impediment to human passage be placed where it should have been in the first place — the guard's van.

It would have been, the flustered man pleads, but for the fact that the train left Dunedin an hour earlier than expected. He had slept in, secure in the knowledge that, like the 'up' service from Cromwell which pulled out around nine, the ex-Dunedin equivalent would do pretty much the same. The guard grimaces and soon he, the flustered man and his bag are negotiating their way down the swaying carriage towards the rear. The train enters the Caversham Tunnel and in the darkness a muffled oath and a clatter of limbs draws attention to the fact that the guard and his now even more flustered charge have taken a tumble while grappling with the heavy bag.

It is a temporary diversion. Soon the red roofs of Dunedin disappear and the train enters the green and pleasant landscape of the Taieri Plains, the first of many stunning physical features of the path followed by the Central Otago train.

In 1927, A. H. Messenger, Acting Government Publicity Officer, undertook a sweeping round trip of the southern lakes of the South Island. Included in his journey was a jaunt on the Central Otago train and he was fulsome in his written praise of nature's bounty on display beyond the carriage window. 'Verdant plain-lands', 'stately poplars and feathery blue-gum', 'a fine plantation of larch trees', 'the tawny mantle of tussock', 'snug homesteads' and 'the glory of blossoming trees' were all wondrous features of a 'landscape of singular beauty and charm'.[1]

Beyond Wingatui Junction, where the Central Otago line heads away from the main trunk, passengers settle back for a pleasant ride, even the flustered man with his luggage crisis solved and those who took a draught of coal smoke and soot through an open window, as the train climbs through a brace of tunnels leading into Salisbury. Just past Taioma the Taieri River appears to the left of the train. The Taieri Gorge looms already, with its distinctive schist outcrops and scrubby vegetation. Parera, a tiny hamlet 30 km out from Dunedin, prompts a friendly matron to announce to whoever can hear that Parera is Maori for 'grey duck'. Bright yellow broom breaks up the uniform rocky greys of the gorge cliffs as the train continues to thread a landscape the friendly matron describes as 'lunar'.

'Only a lunatic would live up here,' a young man adds. That may or may not be so but the people, including schoolchildren, who catch the train at stops like Mount Allan, Little Mount Allan and Christmas Creek seem eager, friendly and quite sane.

At Hindon, in a clearing, the train pulls in for refreshments. It has not long gone 9.10am, the departure time for the complementary service from Cromwell. The express is now 40 km from Dunedin. Hindon township itself is just over 6 km adrift from the railway, down a winding gravel road. This is regarded as the heart of the Taieri Gorge country, although the land closes in even more dramatically further on at Deep Stream, Flat Stream and appropriately, the Reefs. If this is not the heart, it is certainly a constricted artery close to the heart.

The Hindon refreshment rooms have been operated by private lessees from as long ago as 1891, and today's passengers are a lively, hungry bunch, particularly the man with the bulging suitcase, who obviously missed breakfast. Once 537 passengers created a record for a single train and the Hindon staff were run off their feet. The refreshment rooms have a history

The Express takes on water and school kids at Little Mount Allan as the Taieri Gorge closes in.

J.A.T. Terry Photo

AB 694 heads the Express through Hindon. Time for refreshments in a lunar landscape.

J.A.T. Terry Photo

of foot-traffic. The first owner, Mary Ann Gridgeman, dispatched her son to gather up crockery from Dunedin and he walked the entire distance from Hindon. Mrs Gridgeman herself also rode shank's pony to Dunedin on one occasion when provisions were required.

The engine exhaust hammers incessantly as the train heads up the gorge towards the Strath–Taieri Plateau. The rock formations are becoming increasingly exotic, some layered like pancakes, others overhanging the beer-brown river at crazy angles. It's now a long way down as the line edges its way along the cliff and continues to hide itself from time to time in a succession of short tunnels. At Pukerangi the train has fought its way to 250m above sea level, the loftiest point on this stretch, and now there is an easier run through Matarae and Sutton to Middlemarch. Beyond lie the Rock and Pillars, a craggy range crowned by snow on those occasions when the clouds part to provide visibility.

Just out of Middlemarch the train passes the 80 km mark from Dunedin, which now seems to belong to another country. For the next 80 km the train eases up through a vast, arid plain called the Maniatoto. Mountains rise all around — the Rock and Pillar Range to the west, the Taieri Ridge to the east. The line is running parallel to the Pacific Coast, although it's hard to associate this elevated brown desert with anything maritime. Like memories of Dunedin, notions of the ocean belong to a time that seems weeks, rather than hours ago.

After Ngapuna and the settlement of Rock and Pillar, Hyde is the next stop of substance. There are two stops here — Hyde itself and Hyde Township. Hyde is an old gold town and well-known in winter as a centre for the ice-related sports of skating and curling. The town was moved a kilometre en masse when gold was discovered on the site of the original town. It was to become known nationally in 1943 when a fearsome derailment killed 21 passengers and injured 47. Initially many New Zealanders thought the tragedy had occurred on the South Island main trunk. The Central Otago line was a secondary branch and it seemed inconceivable that such a serious accident could befall a friendly, easy-paced spur to a backwater. However, the Central Otago Express was, on that fateful day — 4 June 1943 — travelling at an excessive 70 mph around a curve with a designated speed limit of 30 mph. Already passengers had been tossed around by the lurching of the train and it was little surprise to survivors when it left the tracks in a cutting just south of the town. Access to the crash site proved difficult and it was an hour and a half before rescuers were able to offer assistance.

The driver, who survived, was later declared by a board of inquiry to have been intoxicated when he took over the running of the train, and continued to drink during its doomed passage. Bottles of beer were found in the AB engine (number 782), and the driver was subsequently sent to prison for three years for manslaughter.

In 1939 the drizzle has been swept away by a stiff, bracing breeze. Clouds lift and the Kakanui mountains fill the northeastern horizon. At Kokonga, which means 'a bend' or 'the corner', the Taieri River loops sharply in the flickering sun and the line follows it as the weather settles. Back in July 1908 an extreme weather event wreaked havoc on the line. The snow was over a metre deep at Oturehua and huge rain dumps flooded the Hyde rail yards. Wild winds flattened telegraph poles and the express from Dunedin was stranded. Further up the track at Ida Valley a goods train plunged into a snowdrift and a mixed train, hard on its heels, could not proceed. Passengers were not only inconvenienced, they became virtually hypothermic.

That July was notorious. Later in the month another snowstorm trapped a train near Waipiata and two engines pushing a snowplough came off second best. A huge block of frozen snow derailed the leading loco, closing the line to all traffic for a week.

Ranfurly, the crossing station for the 'up' and 'down' services, is the next stop after Waipiata. It is also where the train stops for a lunch break of 25 minutes. Breaking with the tradition of station refreshment rooms, the railways send passengers across the main street of Ranfurly to find sustenance in the hotel and two nearby private dining rooms. It is a more relaxing means of dining and there is a chance to mingle with the locals should you so desire. Two passenger trains in the town at the same time makes for a significant swelling of the numbers walking the streets of Ranfurly, but there is little hustle and bustle as a result. In fact the relaxed manner of the people of Ranfurly rubs off as passengers revel in the rural pace of life, however temporarily.

Ranfurly is a delightful surprise to first-time travellers. Several passengers terminate their journeys here, to take in the sights, visit Naseby, the old gold town or, in season, skate and curl on the thick ice of Idaburn Dam. Some alight to visit family or friends in the Waipiata Sanatorium. The train has stopped at Waipiata, but for reasons of discretion and unwarranted embarrassment some visitors prefer to remain anonymous, and leave the train further on with everyone else at Ranfurly.

Writer Lawrence Constable, during his travels along the Central Otago line, made particular reference to Ranfurly. Although, to him, the town lacked the atmosphere of the older Otago centres and seemed to offer little, he nonetheless liked the place. Perhaps it was the sense of all-pervading peace, where time stood still, until the two expresses arrived and a quickening of the town's pulse was discernible. Perhaps it was the simple but compelling business of leaving the station precincts to sit down to lunch in a 'rather handsome restaurant'.[2]

Ranfurly has become the major centre on the Maniatoto Plains and enjoyed a building boom in the 1930s when, in the style of the day, many new commercial buildings and houses were constructed in the art deco fashion associated with the re-building of earthquake-devastated Napier.

Ranfurly was an up-country railway town. Its significance could be traced from the arrival of the railway in 1898, when it usurped the importance of the more historic Naseby, 16 km to the north. In 1939 it was even served by its own mixed train, which arrived in a clatter from Dunedin in the early evening. Meanwhile, at the height of the midday sun, the two express engines were serviced, the train crews changed over to travel back along the route from whence they had come, and the influence of the Taieri River, which Lawrence Constable described as being the colour of 'chicken broth', had long gone.

The train driver and fireman were in no hurry. There was even time for two passengers to mount a discussion regarding the origins of the name Ranfurly, in the comparative quiet of the still-stationary express. One man was adamant that the town was named after the Ranfurly Shield, symbol of provincial rugby supremacy, although the other went to some pains to point out that the town was named years before the Ranfurly Shield competition was introduced. It was in fact named after the fifth Earl of Ranfurly, who was Governor-General of New Zealand at a time when the Central Otago railway extended into the region. At one time the town was known as Eweburn. The first man remained adamant as the engine finally whistled across the plains before proceeding.

Lord Ranfurly, Governor of New Zealand, c.1900. The town was named after him, not the shield – although the shield was named after him as well.

ATL-PAColl-5800-50

Through Wedderburn and into the Ida Valley the train, straining under a slightly heavier load (most passengers had dined well at Ranfurly), skirted North Rough Ridge and now the Raggedy Range and Manuherikia River dominated the landscape. Rabbits, a real problem to farmers, scuttled away as the express made its presence felt. Children expressed delight as the cute, furry creatures headed for burrows. The adults knew better.

Dr James Menzies of Mataura, the first superintendent of the Southland province, had released rabbits in 1864, near Bluff. Although his action was by no means the first attempt to acclimatise the creatures for hunting purposes, he had come to be regarded as the man responsible for their introduction. The rabbits spread northwards, devouring grasslands and now Central Otago bore the brunt of their voracious appetites and enthusiastic breeding habits.

Rabbit hunting by railway jigger on the Central Otago line. Could it have become an Olympic event?

ATL-140567-G

Even the railway had been undermined, literally, by the rabbits, who tunnelled into embankments and cuttings and disrupted signalling by unearthing the pegs that confined guide wires. If only the rabbits could have been co-ordinated and utilised during the line's construction — they would have hastened the boring of tunnels on a branch that took forever to complete. At Waipiata they burrowed under the station platform and the subsequent collapse of earth further affected signalling systems.

From the train it's possible to see the occasional wire hairpin from which drying rabbit skins dangle, testament to attempts to keep the pest population in check. It doesn't pay to answer the children's queries as to what the ghoulish objects are. Besides, the train is now picking its way through one of the most desolate, lonely, fascinating stretches on the line. The main road is kilometres away. At Auripo, more isolated than most, the train stops at a station barely bigger than an outhouse. There isn't even a platform and a woman in a tight skirt has the devil's own job clambering on board. Two short tunnels alert those who need to know that Lauder is the next stop, that and the rail bridge across the Manuherikia River just beyond the second tunnel. Then it's on to Omakau, the principal livestock loading station on the line, before the express heads for Alexandra.

At times the physical landscape defies adequate description. Hills, up here, are like no others. They may be described as scalloped, or serrated, as they roll in waves between the light and shadows, but words cannot convey their complexity and uniqueness. Hills stand alone, or form regiments of rock-strewn undulations. Then there are the colours. A subtle light green merges into a yellowy-brown towards the top of many hills. Beyond, the various mountain ranges present a grey-blue blur; the distance between hills and ranges is always much further than the naked eye can appreciate or fathom. The eye plays further tricks when rippled ridges appear to be moving, as if an earthquake is buckling the folds of the land. It is reassuring to realise the movement of the train is creating an optical illusion.

Essentially the line has traced a huge horseshoe curve through Central, and you can blame the Rock and Pillars, Rough Ridge and the Raggedies. It would have cost a fortune and taken a month of Sundays to create a more direct route. As it is, another mountainous slab — the Dunstan Range — dominates the far western horizon and the climb over Rough Ridge into the Ida Valley has crested the highest point on the line.

At around 3pm the train pulls into Alexandra. This is the orchard country with its 'glory of blossoming trees' A. H. Messenger wrote about. Lines of towering poplars complement the fruit trees, and when the stone fruit is ready, 'fruit trains' will start running from Alexandra and the stations further up the Cromwell Gorge, all the way to Dunedin. The Manuherikia meets the mighty Clutha River and locals greet friends and family at Alexandra Station.

Soon the train will be as far from the sea as any train in New Zealand can be.[3]

The Cromwell Gorge closes in as the line changes course dramatically towards the northwest through Clyde. This gorge was once paved with gold during the years of the gold rush, and mining relics and debris line the river bank. At Brewery Creek, a short distance from Cromwell, Hartley and Riley discovered the extensive gold deposits that in 1862 ignited the gold rush and won the discoverers 87lbs of gold and 2000 pounds in hard currency. Now the craggy rocks look down on a desolate region that once hummed with activity.

The Clutha flows sedately as the AB engine coughs and splutters towards the end of the line. The express pulls into Cromwell, population

730, at 4pm, a quarter of an hour late. No one seems to mind. Nor is it of much consequence that the station is located a couple of kilometres this side of the town. A precipice dominates one side of the rail yard, the confluence of the Kawarau and Clutha Rivers catches the eye on the other. In between, as the sun angles away, Cromwell Station is a scene of unhurried disembarkation. The Central Otago Express certainly lives up to its name, as this is the geographic centre of the province and the train, which left Dunedin all those hours ago with the express intention of getting through, has done just that.

Cromwell used to be known as 'the Junction', not because there was a railway branch snaking off through a hole in the rock wall, but because it is where rivers and roads meet. Lake Wanaka awaits to the north, Queenstown and Lake Wakatipu to the west. A family group gathers on the station platform; a family of rabbits bounds away, as the AB disentangles itself noisily from the train.

The express has taken eight hours to traverse the 237 km of the Central Line, from Wingatui Junction, after setting out from Dunedin — good going compared to the time it took to build the line. Years were wasted while the route was chosen. There were as many as seven options to be considered, with a decision finally being made in 1877, although it took another two years before the Railway Construction Act authorised the chosen route and building began. Political prevarication and procrastination, slumps, wars and depression made for stop-start progress and it wasn't until 1921, a whole 42 years later, that the through line was opened.

In the mid-1960s a friend and I travelled across this line. By then the express had become a daily railcar service — a coughing, spluttering Vulcan in the depths of winter — starting at Alexandra. Tom the guard and another Tom, the driver, shared our stony digs, a bed and breakfast arrangement within a stone's throw of the ancient parapet of the old bridge across the Clutha. Phantom Bridge we called it.

It was 5am and mince on toast for breakfast. The temperature was minus nought, our landlady chortled. As we shivered around the breakfast table, with the two Toms sitting opposite, it felt like a foreign country. America, Albania, Northern Scotland, Southern something. We North Islanders were delighted with the mince, slightly spicy, and the positive assurances of Tom the guard and Tom the driver, tasked with getting us through on the Vulcan railcar from Alexandra all the way to Dunedin.

We talked about the rugby as strong tea went down. How Colin Meads should never have been sent off against Scotland and why the All Blacks were just about the best. We chipped in with the revelation that we happened to hail from Colin Meads' hometown — Te Kuiti — where the main trunk split the town in two and friendly, if sometimes direct, people kept an eye out for one another.

A taxi took us to Alexandra Station, the two Toms, my friend and I. At six in the morning it was surprising to find the ticket sellers' window open to possibilities. A middle-aged woman kept a clean window, although her surfaces were freezing to the touch. It was minus six she said, as tickets changed chillblained hands. We took our places on the Vulcan railcar in leather seats as taut as a strong argument. My friend touched a metal fixture and found his skin almost adhering in the cold.

Tom, the driver, manhandled the Vulcan into life and soon we were vibrating as the tired engine coughed. The sun showed no signs of poking through above the hills as the railcar moved like an intruder through the slumbering outskirts of Alexandra, and wan light exposed the Central Otago uplands.

'All tickets please.' The voice in the carriage shadows was like a ghost from the past. It harked back to the sudden, sleep-stirring intrusions of callous guards on the midnight section of the North Island main trunk beyond Ohakune, and a dream-state finally entered after a sleepless sojourn through the central King Country on the Auckland to Wellington express.

'All tickets please.' It was Tom the guard and we were the only passengers, although we thought we had seen an old lady clamber on board in the final ephemeral minutes before departure and pre-dawn. We groped for our tickets, staggered that Tom, the man with whom we had shared digs and mince on toast, was now applying such an officious tone. We did as you did back in 1960s New Zealand, we didn't rock the boat or knock the system, just handed over our tickets to a now thin-lipped, clipping guard who had a job to do. In fact we felt sorry for Tom, decked out in his rough uniform. No body-clinging, heat-retaining garb in the minus-nought situation; instead he looked and sounded cold. We received a perfunctory nod and clipped tickets as the railcar wound through a landscape that had us spellbound and cold.

The loss of the Central Otago line in 1990 has been ameliorated to some degree by the resurrection of the line by the Taieri Gorge Railway from Dunedin, via Wingatui Junction, to Middlemarch and Pukerangi. Beyond that the Otago Rail Trail, where trampers, cyclists and even horse riders can travel along the old embankments and bridges, provides a close encounter with the passage of the old Central Otago Express.

We travelled on the Taieri Gorge train in recent years, a wondrous experience, but still mourn the loss of the line from Middlemarch into the recesses leading to Cromwell, or even Alexandra. The Central Otago Express, or its modern equivalent, could have been as sought-after a journey as the TranzAlpine from Christchurch to Greymouth.

A train of the Taieri Gorge Railway. Looking to the future while rekindling the past.

Graham Hutchins

Notes

Introduction

1 Mark Twain, *Mark Twain in Australia and New Zealand*, Penguin Books, Ringwood, Australia, p. 290.

2 Papers Past, *Star*, 4 November 1891, p. 4.

3 *New Zealand Railways Magazine*, July 1 1927, vol. 2.

4 Papers Past, *Manawatu Herald*, 22 November 1890, p. 3.

5 Robin Hyde (Iris Wilkinson), *New Zealand Railways Magazine*, March 2 1936, vol. 10, p. 41.

6 'Slalom', *New Zealand Railways Magazine*, November 1 1938, p. 31.

7 'Manuhiri', *New Zealand Railways Magazine,* March 1 1937, p. 41.

Chapter 1: Sleepless in Taihape

1 Anthony Trollope, *With Anthony Trollope in New Zealand*, AH & AW Reed, Wellington, 1969, p. 138.

2 W. L. Rapley, *New Zealand Railways Magazine*, December 1 1939, p. 34.

3 'W.F.I', *New Zealand Railways Magazine*, September 1939, p. 19.

4 Lawrence Constable, *Home Territory*, Pegasus Press, Christchurch, 1953, p. 107.

5 W. Hearn Thomas, *New Zealand Railways Magazine*, April 1940, p. 14.

6 H. Hector Bolitho, *With the Prince in New Zealand*, Edwin Sayes, Auckland, 1920, pp. 53-4.

7 Spencer Westmacott, *The After-Breakfast Cigar*, AH & AW Reed, Wellington, 1977, pp. 86-7.

8 Roy Sinclair, *Rail — The Great New Zealand Adventure*, Grantham House, Wellington, 1987, p. 127.

9 Frances Brebner, *New Zealand Railways Magazine*, May 1 1939, p. 25.

10 Jim Henderson, quoting Paul Donoghue in the *Official History of New Zealand in the Second World War, 1939-1945*, Historical Publications Branch, Wellington, 1958. NZ ETC, p. 461.

11 New Zealand Railways Publicity, *New Zealand Railways Magazine.*

12 Audrey B. King, *New Zealand Railways Magazine*, May 1 1939, p. 56.

13 Papers Past, *Evening Post*, 21 July 1908, p. 2.

14 W. H. Lawson, as quoted by Roy Sinclair in *Rail — The Great New Zealand Adventure*, Grantham House, Wellington, 1987, p. 68.

Chapter 2: A prince among travellers

1 W. W. Stewart, *Grand Old Days of Steam*, AH & AW Reed, Wellington, 1967, p. 90.

2 Rupert Brooke, as quoted by H. Hector Bolitho in *With the Prince in New Zealand*, Edwin Sayes, Auckland, 1920, p. 19.

3 H. Hector Bolitho, *With the Prince in New Zealand*, Edwin Sayes, Auckland, 1920, p. 52.

4 *Ibid.*, p. 114.

5 *Ibid.*, p. 213.

Chapter 3: Last stop, Bay of Islands

1 Robin Hyde, *New Zealand Railways Magazine*, September 1 1937, p. 43.

2 Tom Bridges, as quoted by Roy Sinclair in *Rail — The Great New Zealand Adventure*, Grantham House, Wellington, 1987, p. 103.

3 Thomas Bracken, as quoted by Colonel Burton Mabin in *New Zealand Railways Magazine*, September 1 1928, vol. 3, p. 50.

Chapter 4: Taking the waters and the train

1 H. Hector Bolitho, *With the Prince in New Zealand*, Edwin Sayes, Auckland, 1920, p. 35.

2 James Cowan, *New Zealand Railways Magazine*, May 1 1930, vol. 5, p. 25.

Chapter 5: Train to nowhere

1 David More, *Between the River and the Hills*, Wilson & Horton, Auckland, 1976, p. 177.

2 Hamish Keith, *New Zealand Yesterdays*, Readers Digest (NZ), Auckland, 1984, p. 129.

3 Joyce West, *New Zealand Railways Magazine*, September 1 1937, p. 22.

4 *New Zealand Railways Magazine*, May 1 1928, vol. 3, p. 8.

5 Joyce West, *New Zealand Railways Magazine*, September 1 1937, p. 22.

6 *Ibid.*

7 James Cowan, *New Zealand Railways Magazine*, May 1 1929, vol. 4, p. 20.

Chapter 6: Steaming past the mountain

1 D. B. Leitch, *Engine Pass — New Zealand Railways*, AH & AW Reed, Wellington, 1967, p. 36.

2 J.D. Mahoney, *Kings of the Iron Road*, Dunmore Press, Palmerston North, 1982, p. 69.

3 David Walter, *Shakespearean Town under the Mountain — A History*, Dunmore Publishing, Wellington, 2005, p. 145.

4 Joyce West, *New Zealand Railways Magazine*, May 1 1939, p. 21.

5 *Wanganui Herald*, quoted in *New Zealand Railways Magazine*, April 1 1939, p. 59.

6 James Cowan, quoted in *New Zealand Railways Magazine*, May 1 1939, p. 62.

7 James Cowan, quoted by O. N. Gillespie in *New Zealand Railways Magazine*, October 1 1937, p. 9.

8 O. N. Gillespie, *New Zealand Railways Magazine*, October 1 1937, p. 9.

9 Papers Past, *Poverty Bay Herald*, 26 February 1908, p. 5.

Chapter 7: A year before the quake

1 Katherine Mansfield, quoted by Neill Atkinson in *Trainland*, Random House, Auckland, 2007, p. 198.

2 H. Hector Bolitho, *With the Prince in New Zealand*, Edwin Sayes, Auckland, 1920, pp. 112-13.

Chapter 8: South for the summer

1 Papers Past, *Wanganui Herald*, 20 February 1903, p. 5.

2 Mark Twain, *Mark Twain in Australia and New Zealand*, Penguin Books, Ringwood, Australia, p. 287.

3 *New Zealand Railways Magazine*, August 1 1927, vol. 4, p. 11.

Chapter 9: Buller or bust

1 Lois Voller, *Rails to Nowhere: The History of the Nelson Railway*, Nikau Press, Nelson, 1991, p. 247.

2 *Ibid.*, p. 310.

3 *Ibid.*, p. 292.

4 Lawrence Constable, *Home Territory*, Pegasus Press, Christchurch, 1953, pp. 70-71.

Chapter 10: Don't take this train for granted

1 *New Zealand Railways Magazine,* April 1 1940, p. 61.

2 Lawrence Constable, *Home Territory*, Pegasus Press, Christchurch, 1953, p. 84.

Chapter 11: To the rugby on the 'Rocky Island Line'

1 Papers Past, *Evening Post*, 12 May 1893, p. 3.

2 W. H. H. Grapes, *New Zealand Railways Magazine*, December 1 1927.

3 Gordon Slatter, *Football is Fifteen*, Whitcombe & Tombs, Christchurch, 1972, p. 143.

4 *Ibid.*, p. 152.

5 J. M. Grainger, *On and Off the Rails*, Whitcombe & Tombs, Christchurch, 1964, p. 118.

6 Gordon Slatter, *Football is Fifteen*, Whitcombe & Tombs, Christchurch, 1972, p. 152.

Chapter 12: The tawny mantle of tussock

1 A. H. Messenger, *New Zealand Railways Magazine*, January 15 1927, Volume 1

2 Lawrence Constable, *Home Territory*, Pegasus Press, Christchurch, 1953, pp 24-5.

3 A. H. Messenger, *New Zealand Railways Magazine*, January 15 1927, vol. 1.

Bibliography

Atkinson, Neill, *Trainland: How Railways Made New Zealand*, Random House, Auckland, 2007.

Bolitho, H. Hector, *With the Prince in New Zealand*, Edwin Sayes, Auckland, 1920.

Bromby, Robin, *Rails that Built a Nation*, Grantham House, Wellington, 2003.

Churchman, Geoffrey and Hurst, Tony, *The Railways of New Zealand*, Transpress, Wellington, 2001.

Constable, Lawrence, *Home Territory*, Pegasus Press, Christchurch, 1953.

Dangerfield, J. A. and Emerson, G. W., *Over the Garden Wall: The Story of the Otago Central Railway*, Otago Railway & Locomotive Soc. Inc., Dunedin, 1995.

Dollimore, Edward Stewart, *The New Zealand Guide*, H. Wise & Co., Dunedin, 1952.

Frame, Janet, *An Angel at my Table*, Hutchinson, Auckland, 1984.

Frame, Janet, *To the Is-land*, Hutchinson, Auckland, 1983.

Grainger, J. M., *On and Off the Rails: A Railwayman's Story*, Whitcombe & Tombs, Christchurch, 1964.

Green, R. Brett, *Steel Roads over the Mamakus*, self-published, 2002.

Keith, Hamish, *New Zealand Yesterdays*, Readers Digest (NZ), Auckland, 1984.

King, Michael, *New Zealanders at War*, Heinemann, Auckland, 1981.

Leitch, D. B., *Engine Pass: New Zealand Railways*, AH & AW Reed, Wellington, 1967.

Leitch, David & Scott, Brian, *Exploring New Zealand's Ghost Railways*, Grantham House, Wellington, 1995.

Leitch, David & Stott, Bob, *New Zealand Railways: The First 125 Years*, Heinemann Reed, Auckland, 1988.

Mahoney, J. D., *Kings of the Iron Road*, Dunmore Press, Palmerston North, 1982.

More, David, *Between the River and the Hills*, Wilson & Horton, Auckland, 1976.

New Zealand Railfan Magazine (various editions), Triple M Publications, Wellington.

New Zealand Railway and Tramway Atlas, Quail Map Co., Exeter, 1993.

New Zealand Railways Magazine (various editions).

O'Donnell, Barry, *When Nelson had a Railway*, Schematics Limited, Wellington, 2005.

Orr, Russell, *The Hawke's Bay Railway*, Southern Press, Wellington & Dunedin, 1974.

Sargeson, Frank, *Never Enough!*, AH & AW Reed, Wellington, 1977.

Sinclair, Roy, *Rail —The Great New Zealand Adventure*, Grantham House, Wellington, 1987.

Slatter, Gordon, *Football is Fifteen.* Whitcombe & Tombs, Christchurch, 1972.

Stewart, W. W., *Grand Old Days of Steam*, AH & AW Reed, Wellington, 1975.

Trollope, Anthony, *With Anthony Trollope in New Zealand, 1872,* edited by A.H. Reed, AH & AW Reed, Wellington, 1969.

Troup, Gordon (ed.), *Steel Roads of New Zealand*, AH & AW Reed, Wellington, 1973.

Twain, Mark, *Mark Twain in Australia and New Zealand*, Penguin Books, Ringwood, Victoria, Australia, 1973.

Voller, Lois, *Rails to Nowhere: The History of the Nelson Railway*, Nikau Press, Nelson, 1991.

Walter, David, *Shakespearian Town under the Mountain: A History*, Dunmore Publishing, Wellington, 2005.

Westmacott, Spencer, *The After-Breakfast Cigar*, AH & AW Reed, Wellington, 1977.

Websites

www.en.wikipedia.org

www.nzetc.org

www.paperspast.natlib.govt.nz

www.rugbyrelics.com

Acknowledgements

I wish to thank those who contributed material to this book and to credit the assistance of Hamilton City Libraries in research matters. The contribution made by Terry Bishop is also acknowledged with gratitude.

Many reference works were used, but of particular value were the following:

Rails to Nowhere: The History of the Nelson Railway by Lois Voller, *With the Prince in New Zealand* by H.Hector Bolitho and *Home Territory* by Lawrence Constable.

The New Zealand Railways Magazine was another rich source of information. The New Zealand Electronic Text Centre and the Papers Past website of the National Library of New Zealand were further valuable reference points.

The assistance of D.R.Simpson, J.A.T. Terry, J.D. Fitzgerald, Russell Young, Hamilton City Libraries (HCL) and the Alexander Turnbull Library (ATL) in providing photographs is also gratefully acknowledged.